Somerset
Folklore and Customs

Jon Dathen

www.capallbann.co.uk

Somerset Cider Folklore and Customs

Cover design by Paul Mason
Cover - 'The Oldest Apple Tree, the Old Man of the Orchard,'
and all other illustrations by Judy P. Powe.
Back cover photo supplied by Judy P. Powe.

Judy P Powe

Published by:

Capall Bann Publishing
Auton Farm
Milverton
Somerset
TA4 1NE

for

Tara, Jack, Charlie and Tom

'Come to the holy temple of the virgins

where the pleasant grove of apple trees

circles an altar smoking with frankincense'

from '*Aphrodite of the flowers at Knossos*'

(Sappho of Lesbos, Willis Barnstone's trans.)

Contents

Foreword

by John Garland

> '...shimmering magic orchard.
> Sparkling crimson apples
> Green glistening trees.'

Brigid Somerset, Poems

Just recently, I happened upon a limited edition of a model Taunton Cider lorry, which I duly snapped up and presented to the author of this book.

Somerset is synonymous with apples, with a singular type of folklore: wassailing and faery memories. It is believed that a good wassail worship, will conjure laden boughs. I thought this when I read in the Observer, November 10th, 1805, that from a single tree in Eaglesfield, '...there were the astonishing number 5,050 well-grown apples, and about 100 were left upon it, though it is not more than seven inches and a half in diameter at the thickest part of the bole, and is scarcely fifteen feet in height.'

Jon Dathen is both a friend and a contributor to the *West Somerset Reviewer*, which I edit. I feel privileged to welcome such an absorbing apple anthology. Likewise, I feel I must congratulate the publishers, Capall Bann for enriching our interest in this forgotten bower of local folk culture.

There is almost an eternal unravelling peel of poetic and literary apple exotica, but one of my favourites is Robert Frost's *'Unharvested'*:

'For there had been an apple fall

As complete as the apple had given man.

The ground was one circle of solid red.'

Unlike the proverbial apple-cart, the author has plucked an original angle - the folklore of this erotic fruit.

Whether Eve picked an apple from the Tree of Knowledge is a matter of conjecture. However, this lush fruit has coaxed the pens and palettes of myriad artists, poets and writers from the twenty-two varieties mentioned by Pliny to Shakespeare's character Swallow, who invites Falstaff in *Henry V*, to 'a pippin and a dish of caraway.'

From any barrel of apple facts, we may glean that there are 7,500 apple varieties grown worldwide. The apple is a member of the rose family. They are cholesterol, sodium and fat free, and only about 80 calories. Hence the old saying, 'To eat an apple going to bed, will make the doctor beg his bread.'

Somerset Cider is a superb bouquet of enchantments, and altogether different from what the reader might expect.

Cíder

What's the biggest difference
between Somerset and Devon?
Devon doesn't have much yeast.
Somerset has the leaven.

For bushels and bushels of apples
grow on Somerset trees
and the air is full of sweetness
and the sweet attracts the bees.

And I would bet that Somerset bees
make honey that has the green
of lovely winding Somerset lanes
with the most flowers there've ever been

from the buttery yellow of buttercup
and the pale cream of primrose
to the purple richness of thistle
and the wildness of the roe.

So the bees gather the pollen
and place it on the trees
and the cider waits in the apples
on branches as bent as old knees.

They droop heavy with cider apples
and the cider tastes of these,
these things that make up Somerset,
the earth, the hills, the meads.

The things that make cider sparkle.
The things that real cider needs.

Pam Redmond

Introduction

Cider is loved throughout the world. From its heartlands of Somerset, Devon, Cornwall and Herefordshire, it's reached North America, Australia and New Zealand. There are also living cider traditions in Europe, with Normandy in France and Bavaria in Germany deserving especial mention.

In the western counties of England, and in Somerset in particular, it was and for many still is, an integral part of the rural way of life. Over the centuries, folklore and customs have become entwined with the growing of apple trees, the harvesting of the fruit, and the production and consumption of cider. Some of these beliefs and practises are practical, a method of fermentation or a saying recording the best time to plant a tree. Others belong to the realm of magic and pagan belief. These include the propitiation of orchard spirits, ceremonies to ensure a robust harvest, and many little 'somethings,' done, 'just for luck.'

It is the aim of this book to preserve both the history, and all the fun and seriousness, of the folklore and customs connected to cider, its makers and drinkers, through-out the county of Somerset, in the past and the eternal present.

Chapter 1

Applelore

'In the corridors under there is nothing but sleep.
And stiller than ever the orchard boughs they keep
Tryst with the moon, and deep is the silence, deep
On moon-washed apples of wonder.'

John Drinkwater, *Moonlit Apples*

Rhine-side orchards shelter venerable apple ancients, gnarled and coated by lichens, their trunks tipped awry by seasons of flatland winds. They lean their heavy branches on forked sticks, driven deep in peaty soil. The orchard grass grows rich, and contented sheep crop lazily. Blankets of pink and white starry blossoms have graced these aged boughs, and been blown months since to colour the green rhines. Soon, apple-wood will creak again, from the weight of red, green and golden fruit. Before the snow, the cider-making will begin.

There is an old tradition that the crab apple was the first plant created, and that from it, all other life sprang. This wild apple (*Malus sylvestris*) is native to Britain, thriving here since time immemorial.

The druids venerated the apple tree, both as the habitat of their holy plant, mistletoe, and as sacred in its own right. It was from apple boughs that they cut their divining rods, and the centre of the apple revealed their secret. Cut a crab or Cox's in half, and you will discover a perfect pentagram, a five pointed star. This most religious of symbols is sacred to all ancient cultures, from the Chinese to the Native American. It was known as the 'Druid's Foot', since it was the base upon which all druidic teachings were founded.

The druids were an important caste among the ancient Britons. They were priests, lawgivers, diviners, genealogists, poets and historians. Their theocratic rule kept the tribes in stern check.

Somerset was a major centre of druidic colleges and holy places. The Axe valley with its mystic islands was a vast burial ground. A link between this world and the next, a sacred area shaded by orchards.

The cider apple is a cultivated offshoot of the wild. Much closer to its acidic forebear than either cooking or eating apples.

Many theories have been posed for the origins of cider. It is tempting to believe that from earliest times it has been the 'wine' of Somerset. The druids had sacred groves, perhaps cidermaking was part of their monastic life, as it was with their successors, the Benedictine monks of Glastonbury.

Both Celts and druids associated the apple with 'Avalon' or 'Faeryland', an 'Other-world' or plane of reincarnation where there is no age, cold or hunger, summer is eternal and the trees are ever heavy with fruit. Avalon is a Celtic name signifying 'apple isle'. Some have identified it with Glastonbury or other of the islands that rise from the Somerset Levels.

Older traditions place Avalon in the Severn Channel, naming it the 'Green Land of Enchantment'. When the weather conditions are right, beyond or between Steep Holm and Flat Holm it can be glimpsed, rising emerald from the mists.

In Somerset the apple tree is still considered to be a gateway to Faeryland. This is echoed in literature. In the 13th century poem 'Sir Orfeo', Queen Heurodis falls asleep beneath an apple tree. She is abducted by the Faery King and taken to Faeryland:

'There down in shade they sat all three
beneath a fair young grafted tree;
and soon it chanced the gentle queen
fell there asleep upon the green.'

(Tolkien's trans.)

Sir Launcelot has much the same problem in Sir Thomas Malory's 'Morte d'Arthur':

'...and then were they aware of a sleeping knight that lay all armed under an apple tree; anon as these queens looked on his face they knew it was Sir Launcelot.'

Unfortunately for Sir Launcelot he has been bewitched into a deep sleep, and his discoverers are four witch queens led by Morgan le Fay. He too is abducted and imprisoned in an enchanted land.

Morgan le Fay was King Arthur's half sister. She was often portrayed as the Faery Queen of Avalon. After the fateful Battle of Camblan, she bore the dying Arthur to her magical realm, and there among the orchards he awaits Britain's hour of need.

17

All trees possess spirits and the apple is no exception. In Somerset the oldest tree in the orchard is revered as the Apple Tree Man'. To him the wassail offerings are given, and every morning when anyone first leaves the house, he is bowed to as a sign of respect. The Apple Tree Man is also known as 'Lazy Lawrence'or the 'Colt-Pixy'.

Lazy Lawrence is most likely to be seen on a full moon galloping around his orchard, guarding against intruders. He takes the form of a handsome wild colt, with flaring green eyes that transfix apple thieves, leaving them motionless, only to be discovered come morning. He has been known to kick, bite and fly in pursuit of persistent scrumpers. If your conscience is clear and you are far enough away, you may spy him by his moonlit apples.

Be warned though, I have heard Lazy Lawrence described as 'fearsome!'

Lawrence especially favours those that keep to the old ways and leave out offerings for the pixies at night: a dish of cream and a pail of fresh springwater.

A Somerset rhyme pleads:

'Lazy Lawrence let me goo,
Don't hold me summer and winter too.'

While many a Somerset laggard has heard this cry:

'Hey, have Lawrence got your legs?'

The orchard spirits are of course friendly, and protective of the good-hearted. Somerset children when playing catch games

are known to use the apple tree as a sanctuary, calling out the rhyme:

'Bogey, bogey, don't catch me!
Catch that girl in the apple tree!'

It is remembered on Sedgemoor, that a rag-stuffed image or mommet was placed in the boughs of the finest apple tree to ward off evil spirits. This mommet was a symbolic sacrifice to Lazy Lawrence, gaining his protection for the year.

An unusual incident once came to court. A man was charged with shooting at a neighbour who had placed a mommet in an apple tree with its face turned towards his back door. He believed the mommet was there to 'overlook him'. Perhaps his neighbour understandably wished Lazy Lawrence to guard him from such a foul-tempered gun owner.

On Exmoor they say that an apple tree must on no account be planted near a rowan, as one will kill the other.

One tradition practised by the Romans is still alive in Somerset, that of the Name Tree. On the birth of a child an apple tree is planted. The spirit of the tree and the human baby become mystically entwined. The apple spirit cares for the child, who in turn must care for the tree. If a son is far away and his Name Tree is flourishing, he is safe. If the tree wilts, he is sick. If it dies, then he too has passed away.

Some families care for orchards full of relatives and ancestors. In Germany the tradition was to plant apples for boys and pears for girls.

Nowhere in the Bible does it say that the Tree of Knowledge was an apple tree. The tradition that the serpent offered Eve an apple is of northern european origin, suggested by the pagan symbolism of the apple as a fruit sacred to goddesses of the earth and fertility. The Bible lands are not suited to apple cultivation.

The apple has three mythic associations: love, immortality and prophecy. It is important in the mythology and belief of all European peoples.

The Greek god Apollo was often pictured with an apple in his hand. Linking to his role as god of prophecy, inspiration and healing.

The Thebans worshipped Hercules as 'Melius', and offered apples at his altar, in place of the usual sheep.

The goddess Hera was given golden apples on her wedding day by the Earth-Mother Ge. It was these Golden Apples of the Hesperides, which Hercules had to retrieve as the twelfth of his labours.

The Apple of Discord, thrown among the divine guests at the marriage of Peleus and Thetis, was said to have been the cause of the Trojan war. The apple was thrown by Eris, the goddess of strife, twin sister of the war-god Ares.

The Romans held the apple in very high esteem, and considered it sacred to the love goddess Venus. In Sicily today, they are still given as love-gifts. The natural historian Pliny the Elder (23-79 A.D.) recorded twenty-two varieties.

Pomona was goddess of apples and fruit trees. A very ancient Latin divinity, she was honoured by having her own Flamen or 'Bishop', the Flamen Pomonalis. Only the truly native Roman gods had their own Flamens. Pomona possessed a sacred grove near Ostia called the Pomonal.

Ovid in his *'Metamorphosis'* says of her:

'She did not care for woods or rivers, but loved the country-side, and branches, loaded with luscious apples.'

(trans. Mary M. Innes)

Pomona was courted by the rustic gods of the Latin country-side: prophetic farm god Picus, who flies in woodpecker form, and wild Silvanus of the forests, but it was Vertumnus, the god of fruit and seasonal transformation, who won her heart. His feast day was August 23rd, on which he was offered the first fruits of the garden. A practise remembered in the Somerset custom of the Harvest Home.

The apple was also under the patronage of Ceres, goddess of corn and growth.

The Romans imported their own varieties of apple into Britain, and doubtless the rites of Pomona and Vertumnus too.

After the fall of the Roman Empire, the legions withdrew from Britain, traditionally embarking from Brean Down at the mouth of the Axe.

Warriors from Germanic tribes had served with the Romans in Britain. With the legions gone they decided to claim the land they had come to know. Shiploads of adventurers sailed from Germany. Many brought their families and livestock, intending to settle. These were the Saxons, Angles and Jutes. The invaders advanced quickly, founding kingdoms along the East coast, but they suffered a setback when the Britons were temporarily united under King Arthur.

There is still today a russet eating apple produced in Somerset that is known as 'King Arthur's apple'. It is small with a rough skin and is remembered as being a favourite at his court.

The Saxons conquered Somerset in the mid seventh century. Establishing it within the kingdom of Wessex by King Ina's reign (688-726). The dialect of Somerset preserves the Saxon language in surprisingly pure form, retaining archaic words and structures.

The Saxons arrived as pagans with their own gods and traditions. They accepted Christianity before reaching Somerset, but old beliefs linger, even today.

The chief Saxon god was Woden. In an old manuscript, the *Lacnunga*, there is a charm in which Woden advocates the use of apples for healing:

'These nine sprouts against nine poisons.
A snake came crawling, it bit a man
Then Woden took nine glory twigs,
Smote the serpent so that it flew into nine parts,
There Apple brought this to pass against poison,
That she nevermore would enter her house!'

A Somerset 'wisesaw' advocates prevention rather than cure:

'Eat an apple going to bed,
Knock the doctor on the head.'

The Saxons shared the roots of their beliefs with the Norse peoples. In the Scandinavian Eddas, the literary record of their old religion, we read of the goddess Idun, a personification of Mother Earth.

Idun tended an orchard in which the tree of life produced golden apples of immortality. The gods ate her fruit to retain everlasting youth:

> *'The golden apples*
> *Out of her garden*
> *Have yielded you a dower of youth,*
> *Ate you them every day.'*

Richard Wagner (Forman's Trans.)

The Three Norns or Fates kept watch over the Tree of Life, watering it from their sacred well, allowing none but Idun to pluck the apples.

In the *Younger Edda* there is a hidden reference to cider. Idun is referred to in a 'kenning', a poetic device where a god or goddess is indicated by another's name coupled with an attribute of their own. For example Odin becomes 'Victory-Tyr' or 'Hanged-Tyr'. Tyr was another important Norse god.

Idun is called 'Ale-Gefn'. 'Gefn' is a title of the goddess Freya. To distinguish Idun's identity, 'ale' has been added. Idun's link with ale would therefore have been well enough known to enable any listener to ascertain exactly who the poet was describing. The ale linked to Idun, goddess of the Golden Apples can only have been cider.

Apples and immortality, cider and long-life go hand in hand. Could the mysterious elixier of immortality have been cider?

To the Saxons, apples were a staple of diet. Their world was without tea, coffee, potatoes or tobacco. Cider was drunk, apples were eaten fresh, roasted, or transformed into preserves and sauces. Saxon towns often had separate apple markets for buying and selling the different varieties. The importance of the apple is emphasised by this quote from the Coronation Benediction of the Saxon kings:

'May the almighty bless thee with the blessing of heaven above, and the mountains and the valleys, with the blessing of Grapes and Apples. Bless, O Lord, the courage of this Prince, and prosper the work of his hands; and by Thy blessing may this land be filled with Apples, with the fruit and dew of heaven, from the top of the ancient mountains, from the Apples of the eternal hills, from the fruits of the earth and its fullness.'

The belief that magical power resided in the apple survived into the seventeenth century. The fruit was mentioned at several witch trials as a medium for spells.

On the 15th November 1657, Jane Brooks of Shepton Mallet gave Richard Jones an apple in return for some bread. He was taken ill, losing his power of speech, but subsequently recovered and gave evidence. Jane was executed at Chard in 1658. Her sister Alice Coward was also tried for witchcraft, first at Castle Cary and then at Shepton Mallet. She was said to have croaked like a toad.

In 1658 a Yeovil witch was sentenced to death on the evidence that she had bewitched a young boy. The witch had asked the boy for a portion of his bread. He refused and she bewitched him, causing him to lift into the air and fly three hundred yards. She had given him an apple to eat.

The witches of Brewham Forest, Wincanton were brought to trial in 1664. They testified that to bewitch their enemies they used apples previously blessed by their coven master, whom they addressed as 'Robin'.

To dream of apples brings success in business, signals a lover's faithfulness, and is an omen of long life.

Chapter 2

Ciderlore

'Good luck to the hoof and the horn, Good luck to the flock and the fleece, Good luck to the growers of corn, With the blessings of plenty and peace.'

(Traditional cider toast)

Somerset tradition claims cider history dates from before the time of Christ.

The introduction of cider has also been attributed to the monks of Glastonbury Abbey. The monks certainly produced cider, and the area is prime orchard land. A monastery orchard was known as a 'pomerium'.

Another theory is that the Normans imported cidermaking from Normandy. This goes against the grain. Traffic across the channel was always two-way, and it seems more likely that the hard-drinking Normans invaded to acquire the recipe.

Some of the earliest literary mentions of cider occur in Saxon herbal manuscripts, where its medicinal qualities are noted.

The word cider has a Hebrew origin, deriving from 'shekhar' meaning 'strong drink'. The Greeks adopted the word

as 'sikera'. From them it passed into Mediaeval Latin, then to Old French as 'Cisdre', and on into modern English.

It is hard to believe that the Hebrews did not have cider in Biblical times. Consider this quote from the Song of Solomon 2:5:

'Stay me with flagons, comfort me with apples: for I am sick of love.'

(King James trans.)

Scholars disagree as to whether apples are mentioned in the Bible. The phrase 'apple of my eye' is used many times, but it is a poetic paraphrase introduced by the King James translation. The words in the original Hebrew make no mention of fruit. Other passages use the word *'tappuwach'*. It is rendered as 'apple'. Which fruit it actually signifies is not known. The apricot, orange and quince are all candidates.

King Solomon may well have dined upon apples. The Jerusalem aqueduct he built was constructed of Mendip lead. Pheonician and other Eastern merchants traded with the ancient British for their minerals, travelling a coastal route around France and Spain. Such enterprising businessmen would have tried exporting other products. If cider was produced at that time, prize barrels would have found their way to Solomon's court.

Somerset tradition remembers Joseph of Arimathea trading in Cornwall for tin and on Mendip for lead. On many of his visits Our Lord and his mother accompanied him. Whether St. Joseph and his guests landed at Watchet and travelled overland, sailed up the Axe past Uphill, or along the Parrett, they would have been welcomed and treated to local fayre.

'Scrumpy' or 'scrump', the local names for rough dry farmhouse cider, are English words derived from 'scrimp' meaning 'withered'. A reference to the apples used.

Somerset farmhouse cider is a very different drink to the 'fizzy stuff' produced by the big breweries. It is still and strong, an amber or amber-red colour. All the natural fruit sugars are fermented out, leaving next to no sweetness. Traditionally no water, additives, flavourings, sugars or artificial yeasts are added. Its strength can reach 9% alcohol. The uninitiated are advised not to drink more than a half pint per session. This is the cider that has been a vital part of Somerset life since Saxon times.

In times past, cider pervaded the social fabric of Somerset. Every farm had its orchard and produced its own cider. Farmers in isolated areas such as the Brendon Hills, doubled as innkeepers, and their home-produced beverage was naturally cider.

Farmhouses either had cellars for the storing and making of cider, or among the outbuildings there would be a cider house, also called the 'wring house' or 'pound house'. This was often a specially constructed two storey building. All means would be used to ensure a cool environment could be maintained inside. Trees were planted to provide shade. Windows were kept to a minimum. The floor was of cobble or flag stones, and the roof was insulated with straw. The top floor was an apple loft or 'tallet', where the apples were stored before cidermaking commenced.

Within the cider house walls were huge barrels of cider, and all the equipment for making it. Here on a Sunday morning, after the farm chores had been done, the farmer, his neighbours, friends and workers, would gather, to drink, swop stories and sing the old songs. The smell of tobacco in clay pipes would have been rich, but not as rich as the smell of cider straight from the cask. It was drunk from a large pottery mug, graced with a suitable motto, such as the Farmers' Prayer:

'Let the Wealthy and great
Roll in splendour and state
I envy them not I declare it
I eat my own lamb
My own chickens and ham
I shear my own fleece and I wear it
I have lawns I have bowers
I have fruits I have flowers
The lark is my morning alarmer
So jolly boys now
Here's God speed the plough
Long life and success to the farmer'

The cider mug had two or three handles to ease its passing around the company. All drank in good fellowship from the same vessel, but first an offering was made. An elder of the company would pour a brimming cup of cider to the earth, exclaiming, 'A drop for wold Heark'.

This libation gives thanks to the Earth, producer of cider.

'Wold' is Somerset for 'old', and 'Heark' minus the dialect 'H' is 'Eark', a Saxon name for the Earth goddess, as witnessed by this invocation for fertility from the *Lacnunga* manuscript:

'Erce, Erce, Erce, Mother of Earth'
May the All-Wielder, Ever Lord grant thee
Acres a-waxing, upwards a-growing
Pregnant with corn and plenteous in strength'

This custom has survived to the present day. On camping trips as a teenager, a friend always insisted we pour a cup of cider on the earth to appease her, otherwise she would claim her right by causing a spill. Erce got her dues and no spillage was ever reported. He was right!

When cider was drunk by workers in the fields, it was often the last drop that was offered.

At one time a farmworker's wage was one shilling and a half gallon of cider a day. Boys were given a quart.

At haymaking and harvest the cider flowed in unlimited quantities. Before the coming of machines, extra labour was vital to the success of these tasks, and a farmer's livelihood rested upon whether he could attract the necessary help. If his cider was good and his barrels plentiful, the labourers would queue.

Each morning before work, the men would assemble at the cider house to receive their ration. Each had a vessel in which to carry the precious liquid. Some swore by the 'owl' or 'hedgehog', an apple-shaped earthenware jar, carried by a thong. An owl stood at least ten inches high, held a gallon or half-a-gallon, and was reputed to keep the cider cooler. Others carried 'firkins', small wooden barrels. They mostly held a half gallon, but did vary. The smaller ones held as little as half a pint and were known as 'goose eggs'. Firkins were hard to break and could be carved with mottos or initials. Very old firkins were sometimes made of leather. By 1890 owls were rare.

Stone jars were also popular, and were wrapped in protective withy baskets to withstand rough handling in the fields. These too carried the half gallon ration.

Every man owned a cow horn drinking cup. Its rim and base were of silver or other fine metal. These cups held less than a quarter of a pint.

The inclusion of a cider ration in workers' wages was made illegal by extension of the *Truck Acts* to agriculture in 1878. In 1908 a government Select Committee found the custom still strong. Many farmers continued it unofficially, but by the end of the Second World War they were few.

By the Inn fireside other equipment was used. On cold nights cider was drunk piping hot with ginger, and sometimes cut half-and-half with gin. It was either heated by plunging a red hot poker in, or over the fire in a strange contraption that resembled a large candle-snuffer. More commonly a cider shoe was used. A brass, tin or copper vessel, shaped like a boot, with a lid and handle. It was snuggled under the coals of the vast open fire, until the cider bubbled.

Cider vessels, equipment and mugs were passed down in families, becoming heirlooms.

Traditional orchards have an ambience all their own. The trees stand at least thirty feet apart, sometimes positioned in rows, often seemingly planted sporadically. This gives 40 trees to the acre, and each acre produces around four to six tons of apples. Modern bush orchards can produce between eight and ten tons. Between the old style trees, lush grass thrives. Their branches spread high, reaching twenty to thirty feet into the sky. In low lying districts, the soil was built up into raised ridges on which the trees could be planted. When the fields flooded in winter, the dips or 'grykes' between the ridges would fill with water. In very wet areas each standard tree would be planted on its own mound of soil, which became a little island when the waters came.

Many traditional standard trees crop really well one year, the 'on year', and then poorly the next. This is known as 'biennialism'. In the past this was sometimes due to the apples being beaten down with sticks. The new buds were destroyed, leaving the tree unable to crop the next year.

Standard or 'traditional' trees blossom for ten to fifteen years before cropping fully. A farmer will 'put down' a young orchard and use the ground as arable until the trees mature. It used to be said that a man must lay an orchard for his grandchildren, not himself.

At Burrowbridge on Sedgemoor it is recorded that apple trees were planted in the withy beds. By the time the beds became exhausted a mature orchard was in place.

Somerset cider is traditionally produced from varieties of apples known as 'bittersharps', high in both tannins and acids. 'Bittersweets' are blended in for sweeter cider. Sometimes cookers and eaters, more properly known as 'sharps' and 'sweets', were added.

Cider apples have their own lore. Some varieties are legendary, some just for their names. Kingston Black is famed throughout Somerset, originating in the Quantocks village Kingston St. Mary. It is widely held as the best apple, producing a cider, rich, deep and strong.

Another legend is Cocky Gee, once known as the 'King of Ciders'. Imported from Ireland in the eighteenth century, its true name was 'Coccagee', or 'Goose Turd' in Gaelic. In old English 'Cocky Gee' means 'Saucy Fellow', an apter translation.

Cocky Gee is now lost. Perhaps somewhere in Somerset a tree remains from which the variety can be revived.

Tom Putt, known as the cottager's apple was a domestic favourite. Developed by the Eighteenth century Devon landowner Sir Thomas Putt, it could be eaten, baked for dessert, or turned into good cider.

Other Somerset varieties include: Sweet Jersey, Norman, Cap O'Liberty, Quarrendon, Orange Pippin and Somerset Red Streak. Newer ones are the Dunkerton Late Sweet and Yarlington Mill.

Many farmers made their ciders out of whatever apples were at hand, merrily mixing varieties. Others worked on specific blends. Some kept the varieties sacred, making pure Kingston Black or Cocky Gee. These unblended ciders are now known as vintage ciders.

Often a farmer would make several types of cider from different trees. Rougher cider for the labourers, and fussed over, quality cider for himself and his house guests.

One tree in the orchard was sometimes found to make the best cider, and the farmer would jealously guard its apples, using them only for his own cider, venerating the tree as the ''Strong Tree' or the 'Best Tree'.

Local cider has its own unmistakable taste. Cider apples grown in Taunton Vale make cider without the rich peaty note of cider from the Levels. Yearly weather will vary the cider too. A hot summer and cold winter is deemed best.

Orcharding is an art. 'Gribble' or pip grown trees, known as 'wildings', tend to be wild cards, never resembling their parent. Sometimes, varieties are discovered by accident. Yarlington Mill began as a wilding. The old farmers used to let wildings spring up, in case any of them turned out to be a useful variety.

All orchard trees are grafted or budded. A root stock is grown from the more virile crab apple or a wilding. Onto this, shoots or buds from the desired variety are joined. These then grow as part of the stock but retain fully the nature of their parent. So all trees of any variety, are essentially the same tree.

Seven to eight acres of orchard was average for a three-hundred acre farm.

Twenty-one bushels of apples produce approximately one hogshead of cider, that's 54 gallons. One bushel is equivalent to 8 gallons. Occasionally a quantity of apples was measured in bushels, similarly it is possible to have a pint of elderflowers, in other words, the amount of elderflowers that will fit into a pint glass. Measured by weight, it can take 20lbs of apples to produce one gallon of cider.

Somerset was once a sea of orchards. In 1894 it is estimated that there were 24,000 acres of cider orchard. In 1973 it was down to 2,500, but the acreage is growing again.

'And a little more cider won't do us no harm,'

(Wassail Song)

The health giving properties of cider are legion. To achieve full benefits, half pint a day should be drunk, and the cider should be good strong dry Somerset farmhouse cider.

Cider prevents and cures rheumatism and gout. It purifies the blood and is an aid to digestion. The malic acid in cider neutralises any excess of chalky matter caused by eating too much meat.

The regular cider drinker will never suffer from calculus (kidney stones or gallstones).

Cider in which horse-radish has been steeped is helpful for dropsy (oedema or water retention) sufferers.

An older remedy for scalds and sprains was 'verjuice', fermented crab apple juice.

Cider drunk piping hot with ginger and burnt toast floating in it makes a fine cold cure.

The typhoid bacillus cannot live for long in apple juice. Drinking water of doubtful quality is improved by mixing with cider, but why spoil good cider by mixing it with impure water?

Of course, drinking too much cider results in drunkenness, and even a little on an empty stomach can start the unwary wobbling. A retired Somerset farm labourer from Weston-Super-Mare explained;

'In the fifties we still drunk cider in the fields until it was comin' out of our ears, but then we ate with it, big hunks 'o bread 'an cheese. On an empty stomach it's deadly stuff. We didn't have no accidents 'cos of drunkenness, we worked it off. The cider kept us goin'. After a break we rushed back to work like new men.'

Cider does grant a flow of energy to the weary. He went on, 'To be drunk on cider is like being drunk on nothing else. There's somethin' in cider that really sends you if you over do it. See things you do. Blows 'yer veins too, you get a big red nose, spread all over 'yer face.

There's always some that take it too far. Some of they boys lost everything, jobs, wives, and cared for nothing but the cider, drinkin' p'raps ten to twelve pints a day, an' that was the old strong farmhouse brew. Go mad in the end they would. We'd say of anyone who weren't quite right, that they'd, 'gone to Wells', 'cos that was where the sanitarium was, where the worst cases ended up.

In the fifties and sixties in Weston there weren't no crime, just a bit of drinkin' and fight'n.' They tourists from Birmingham did used to come down and boast they could swallow anything. 'Course once they started on the cider they couldn't handle it. After twelve the police'd send out a wagon to pick their bodies out 'o the ditches.

Still, on a Sunday morning, if you get out to they cider farms, the old boys roll up with their jugs or barrels in their wheelbarrows, and get 'em filled with their weekly ration. Sixteen gallons some of 'em get, and they get through it too! Most have a glass and a natter with old cronies there and then. Highlight of their week it is.'

Chapter 3

Cider Chronicles

*'An' there's no drinks like the old drinks,' cried the smith with
enthusiasm. 'Not for comfort and good friendship.'*

(*The Book of Simple Delights*, Walter Raymond)

In 1230 Bishop Jocelin of Bath received a grant mentioning
cider presses. Monastic cider making must have begun long
before. Monks were jollier in those days! The cider was sold to
increase Abbey revenues. By 1243 it was making a tidy profit
for the Bath Bishopric.

King John was a contemporary of Bishop Jocelin. He reigned
from 1199 to his death in 1216. We read in Foxe's '*Book of
Martyrs*', published 1563, that:

'This ague he (King John), *encreased by eating Peaches and
drinking of new Ciser, or as we call it Sider.'*

This image of King John agrees with Somerset folk-memory of
him as a 'jolly sort', fond of good hunting and grand feasting.

It was King John who inaugurated the Reeve's Feast at North Curry. Every Boxing Day, a huge mince pie bearing his effigy was ceremoniously eaten, and his health toasted:

> *'To the immortal memory of King John*
> *To the real Jack o' Knapp*
> *To the real Jack o' Slough.'*

The Jacks were the presiding officials of the feast.

While two candles weighing a pound each burned, the feasters could eat and drink as much as they pleased. The tradition was continued until the 1930's.

King John also helped to keep Somerset throats from drying, by granting the charter for Bridgwater Fair in 1200. Good old King John!

Before printing became established in England by William Caxton in 1477, literary mentions of cider are rare. Confusingly, in early sources it is often referred to as 'wine'.

Cider almost makes an appearance in Shakespeare's 'A Midsummer Night's Dream'. Puck, his literary pixie confesses:

> *'Sometimes I lurk in a gossip's bowl. In very likeness of a roasted crab.'*

Puck is playing pranks on a drinker of the old beverage 'lambswool'. Spiced ale or cider in which roast apples float.

The seventeenth century saw wars raging across Europe. England rejoiced in being an island nation. With imports of wine becoming scarce, cider rose in esteem, becoming a drink of the royal court.

Inspired by renaissance freedom of thought, the new scientists were eager to publish their knowledge. Agriculture and cider production were ripe subjects.

Dr John Beale wrote on Herefordshire Orchards in 1657. He considered cider, ' ... *the richest, strongest, the most pleasant and lasting wine that England yet yields...* '

John Worlidge's '*Vinetum. Brittannicum*' was published in 1678. A truly comprehensive book on orcharding, cider-making, machinery and methods. He declared cider, 'the most transcendant liquor this Nation affords'.

In 1685 Somerset was traumatised by the Duke of Monmouth's uprising. Crowning himself 'King Monmouth' in Taunton market, he led hordes of eager but inexperienced county men against King James' crack troops.

'King Monmouth' was believed to be a Protestant Divine King. His purpose was to rest the crown from the Catholic James II.

The rebellion culminated in the Battle of Sedgemoor. Monmouth's surprise night attack on the royal army came close to success. The royal troops had been guzzling Zoyland cider and were 'fuzzy'. However, the superior arms and numbers of the royal army eventually prevailed. The Somerset men never surrendered, fighting at the last with only billhooks and scythes against muskets and sabres.

The defeated boys and men of Somerset, mostly weavers and yeoman farmers were tried at the 'Bloody Assizes' of Judge Jeffries. Some were transported, at least 150 were hung drawn, quartered, and their tarred remains displayed in their home villages.

In 1686, John Aubrey's 'Remains of Gentilisme', a record of rural belief and folk customs, detailed the Somerset 'wassail' ceremony, revealing a vigorous tradition:

' ... they goe with their Wassell-bowle into the orchard and goe about the trees to blesse them, and putt a piece of tost upon the roots in order to it.'

Seventeenth century transport left much to be desired. There were no railways or canals. Roads were boggy and often indistinguishable from the surrounding countryside, especially in the more rural districts.

In 1697, Miss Celia Fiennes journeyed through Somerset on horseback, and recorded her impressions in a diary. To travel at all was a sign of wealth. In a woman it revealed an adventurous spirit. She wrote:

'In most parts of Somersetshire it is very fruitfull for Orchards, plenty of apples and peares, but they are not curious in the Planting the best sort of fruite which is a great pitty, being so soone produced and such quantetyes, they are likewise as Careless when they make cider - they press all sorts of Apples together, else they might have as good sider as in any other parts, even as good as the Herrifordshire - they make great quantetyes of Cider, their presses are very large, so as I have seen a Cheese as they call them which yielded 2 hoddsheads - they pound their apples, then lay fresh straw on the press, and on that a good lay off Pulp of the apples, then turne in the ends of the straw over it all round and lay fresh straw, then more apples up to the top'.

That was just twelve years after the Monmouth rebellion. Minds would not have been focused on the niceties of cidermaking. Either that or the farmers gave the aristocratic Miss Fiennes, some of the 'rough' to drink.

In 1706, John Philips finished his monumental poem '*Cyder. A Poem in Two Books*'. Never had the praises of cider been sung in such elegaic style. The poem ran to over 1400 lines. At that time it was probably the longest complete poem in the English language.

John Philips chose to devote such a composition to cider, because he felt it his duty. He wished to enshrine in verse the patriotism he felt for his native land and its natural produce.

Although born in Bampton, Oxfordshire, he had strong family links in Herefordshire, a strong cider county. His father was Arch-deacon of Salop, or Shropshire, another shire with cider traditions. These places, deep in orchards, inspired him.

'*Cyder. A Poem*', is classical in form, modelled on the 'Georgics' of Virgil. John Philips was a scholar of classical poetry and the great English bards: Chaucer, Spencer and Milton. He felt that English poetry had declined, and intended to take it back to its heights, using ancient meters and mythological metaphors.

If read with diligence, his painstaking poem has real beauty. It leads the reader through every aspect of the cider process and farming year, excelling in descriptions of rural life:

'*The farmer's toil is done; his cades mature*
Now call for vent, his lands exhaust permit
T' indulge awhile. Now solemn rites he pays
To Bacchus, author of heart-cheering mirth.

44

His honest friends, at thirsty hour of dusk,
Come uninvited; he with bounteous hand
Imparts his smoking vintage, sweet reward
Of his own industry; the well-fraught bowl
Circles incessant, whilst the humble cell
With quavering laugh, and rural jests resounds.
Ease, and content, and undissembled love
Shine in each face; the thoughts of labour past
Encrease their joy.'

Describing the Royalist party in the Civil War, Philips summons to mind Monmouth's rebellion:

'The Cyder-land obsequious still to thrones,
Ahorr'd such base disloyal deeds, and all
Her pruning-hooks extended into swords,
Undaunted, to assert the trampled rights
Of monarchy; but, ah! successless she,'

John Philips had always suffered bad health. In 1707 he went to Bath, seeking restoration from asthma and tuberculosis. There he may have tasted Somerset cider.

Passing away in 1708, he was interred in Hereford Cathedral, and merited a monument in Poets Corner, Westminster Abbey.

'*Cyder*'was translated into Italian.

It gained wide popularity in Somerset. Edmund Smith penned a verse in memory of John Philips, including the line:

'Thee on the Po kind Somerset deplores,'

Author Daniel Defoe started life as a London merchant, but a great part of his business was done in Somerset. He had relatives in Martock, and knew Yeovil, Bristol, Bridgwater and Minehead.

Defoe was twenty-five years old when he rode with Monmouth's rebels at the Battle of Sedgemoor. He escaped both the slaughter, and the vengeance loosed on the survivors.

In his *'Tour Through England and Wales'*, published 1724, Defoe described Somerset, championing cider as, *'So very good, so fine so cheap ...'*

By 1750 the cider boom was beginning to wane as imported liquors again flooded the market. Cider retreated to its heartlands: Somerset, Devon, Cornwall, Gloucester, Hereford and Dorset.

The 1763 government tax on cider was welcomed with scorn. For every hogshead, the cider maker payed the government four shillings. The excisemen were given access to enter and search private homes.

William Pitt the Elder fought the tax, declaring, *'Every man's house is his castle.'*

In 1766 the tax was repealed. Cidery public celebrations occurred in market places all over Somerset.

When the famous diarist Parson Woodforde travelled to his curacy in Babcary, to preach on January 15th 1764, he was *'...rung into the Parish by Mr. John Bower's order, who gave the Ringers a pail of Cyder on purpose to ring me into the Parish.'*

On December 3rd 1767, Woodforde found cause to criticise his servant Luke Barnard '... *He is a willing fellow, but indolent and too fond of cyder*'.

A Somerset gentleman, John Billingsley, published in 1795 his *'General View of the Agriculture of the County of Somerset'*. He gives advice and helpful recipes for sweet and dry ciders.

Praising the cidermaking of Somerset farmers, he comments, *'But the method of doing this they endeavour to keep a profound secret'*.

Times have not changed!

During the Napoleonic Wars 1790-1815, England again became an island unto itself. Foreign trade ebbed, and cider was shipped from the west to the wine-starved palates of the cities.

Once foreign trade resumed, cider was marginalised. The Victorian era, with its passion for 'gentility', saw it once again confined to its homelands.

The agricultural depression in the latter nineteenth century left many orchards untended. The rural poor flocked to the industrial cities. Mechanisation of farming processes meant that their labour was not required. Those who stayed on the land clung to the old traditions, and their cider.

The national trauma of the Great War changed the face of the countryside, shattering communities and families. Post 1918 England was a vastly different place. Many customs of Merry England had become fond memories.

The great Somerset chronicler of the pre-war years was Walter Raymond (1852-1931). His tender novels of the Somerset countryside are a vibrant record, but his essays are an outstanding achievement. In *'The Book of Simple Delights'*, *'The Book of Crafts and Character'*, and *'Gossip Corner'*, his pen lovingly painted images of country ways that even then were passing away. These delights, he crafted at Withypool on the edge of the Quantocks, between 1906 and 1914. Being books of Somerset, cider features consistently.

'He took the cup and held it from him almost at arm's length. Then, with a slight quiver of the wrist, he spilt it may have been a teaspoonful upon the ground.

'Here's luck!' cried he.

'Zame to you'. replied Mrs. Chedsey.

His red, weather-beaten face was a picture, as the blue cup slowly lifted whilst he drank.'

(*The Book of Simple Delights*, 1906)

Walter Raymond fondly referred to Somerset as 'Ciderland'.

In his eighty years Raymond became a part of the countryside, and as much a 'character', as anyone he wrote about. Much loved, he was that rare being, a man of letters, and of the people. He confessed, '...my heart was always in the fields and with the folk'.

Unlike many chroniclers of folklore and dialect in the years before the Second World War, Raymond lived among the villagers, accepted as part of the community, and privy to secrets whispered only to the true native. There is no condescension in his writing.

'Now a good warm vire, a vew friends an' a drop o' cider be the ruination o' silence.'

(Gossip Corner, 1907)

Part of Raymond's magic was his mystic communion with nature, shown as he writes of orchard trees in his essay 'Cidermaking':

'Even in leafless winter their moss-clad branches, with the sunlight from a clear, frosty sky glinting between the twigs to melt the dripping rime, are full of colour. Sometimes high up there grows a bough of mistletoe, green as a bush in summer and spangled with berries that look like pearls.'

(The Book of Crafts and Character, 1907)

Raymond inspired a younger generation of folklorists to record the dialect and customs of Somerset. J. A. Garton counted himself a 'disciple'. He recorded dialect faithfully and loved his subject:

'...Dost thee know what thic thur wur used var?'

Farmer Dibble pointed to a small bottle-shaped basket with one flat side and two little legs. The Boy owned that he didn't.

'Tha's what th'd'call a huckmuck, an' 'tiz what we did use to straain the muther out o' the cidur wi'.'

He did know that muther was the slimy jelly that sometimes forms in cider.'

(Glowing Embers from a Somerset Hearth, 1936)

The 'Somerset Folk Movement' dedicated itself to recording the 'Old Ways' of the county, and thrived until the outbreak of the 1939-1945 war. W. G. Willis Watson and Dr. John Read, both published by the Somerset Folk Press, recorded ciderlore:

'... 'haymaking' commences, and men and women come with long rakes and the waggons haul away huge loads to the corner down by the holly bush, and all have dinner under the elm tree, and the cider is passed round, and pipes smoked...'

(The Land of Summer, W. G. Willis Watson)

The Somerset Yearbook, which circulated widely from 1921-1939, printed many fascinating snippets of cidery information, before fading at the onset of war.

Somerset was known in cricket circles as 'The Cider County'. When the legendary Sammy Woods, Somerset captain 1894-1906, played Surrey, voices would call, 'Give 'em cider Sammy!'

The world has stood on its head over the last fifty years, but Somerset is eternally 'Ciderland', where farmhouse cider is made in the old way, and drunk as it always was, cool from the barrel, by a great wood fire.

Chapter 4

The Cidermakers' Almanac

'Ha, tidden the cider', said long Jims Matravis, with the grave shake of the head which comes of conviction. 'Cider's a thing no man can ha too much o'. Tidden the cider.'

(*Two Men o' Mendip*, Walter Raymond 1898)

'Everything in its place, and a place for everything', could well be applied to the folk calendar. The festival customs of England chiefly celebrate seasonal changes and important phases in the agricultural and pastoral year.

To understand the fond place these old festivals hold in the hearts of country people, we must travel back in time.

Merry England was a rural country. The towns had proportionately small populations. The majority of workers toiled in the fields and forests. Only luxury goods were imported. The Industrial Revolution had yet to make the farm labourer redundant on the land, and drag him into the sweatshops of the cities.

The farming year was essentially the same as it had been since the Stone Age. Summer followed winter, and winter

followed summer. The ancient pagan feasts celebrated each season and gave thanks for the harvest. With the incoming of Christianity many of these holy days were granted saints' names.

The Christian church made every effort to fit in with the customs of their converts, often taking over the organisation of pagan feasts. A good example is Christmas Day, originally a celebration of the Winter Solstice, the sun's rebirth after the longest night.

In ancient Rome, Christ shared his birthday with Sol Invictus the Unconquerable Sun, and Mithras the Lord of Light. The Bible gives no precedent for celebrating the birth of Our Lord on December 25th. It was just convenient to fit it within the pagan feast.

Jesus Christ became the new Sun, and through the cycle of the year, like so many other deities, he is born, sacrificed, and resurrected.

Other festivals survived outside the Church, passed down whisper to ear, through the years. In minds uncluttered by education, the written word, television or radio, traditional knowledge in the form of folksongs, tales, legends and lore was cherished, and preserved in incredible detail.

The ancient labourer never received four weeks holiday a year. Farm work permits no rest. Even on the sabbath the animals have to be fed. Every feast, whether a Saint's day or a Fair day, was a boon. Once the chores were done, rest or revelry was allowed. The old celebrations were loved as welcome respites. The Harvest Home meant not only a good party, but that the intense labour of harvest was past, and the crops stored safely away.

The Cidermakers' Almanac is a journey through the cidermakers' year, recording customs and sayings in context of their place in the traditional cidermaking process.

On no one farm would all of these practises or sayings have been known or carried out. Many cidermakers keep one custom alive religiously and disregard others.

Modern production methods have rendered a lot of the old lore obsolete, but it is by no means extinct.

The dates of traditional observances such as the wassail ceremony, vary from district to district, but all wassails will take place within a few weeks of each other. Anciently the New Moon or Full Moon would have been chosen. More modernly, weekends are picked for convenience.

Further confusion was caused by the calendar change in 1752. This reform had its origin in 1582, when Pope Gregory XIII introduced the Gregorian calendar to Catholic countries. This was an update of the Julian calendar formulated by Julius Caesar. The Gregorian calendar was essentially the same, but the earlier Julian version had miscalculated the number of leap years. By the sixteenth century it was out by ten days.

Protestant England resisted the change until 1752, when eleven days were omitted between the 3rd and the 14th of September.

The English in the main refused to budge and continued to feast on the 'old' days, hence Wassail Night is often 'Old Twelfth Night', the evening of January 17th in one village, while near neighbours 'Apple-howl' on the night of January 5th 'New Twelfth Night.'

Lady Day (25th March) - Midsummer Day (24th June)

Lady Day marked the beginning of spring, and was an English quarter day, when property leases and land changed hands.

Cider was of such importance to the farmer, that to be able to predict a good crop of cider apples set his heart at rest. There was a rhyme to help:

'Blossom in March - got to search;
Blossom in April - only a hatvul;
Blossom in May - come to stay.'

Cuckoo Day, April 15th was known in Somerset as 'Cuckoo Fair Day'. It was on this day that the cuckoo should arrive. It was said that if he came earlier, frost would destroy the blowth in the orchards and ruin the apple crop.

By the middle of May the orchards are a mass of pink and white blossom, and in a fine year will be just beginning to set fruit.

The days around the 19th of May are crucial for the orchardist. There is often a 'Little Winter'. This cold spell brings a late frost to threaten the cider apples. Such dark doings must have a cause, and the Somerset legend blames St. Dunstan, Saxon saint, monastic reformer and Baltonsburgh man.

St. Dunstan brewed beer and was deeply concerned that the men of Somerset drank nothing but cider, turning their noses up at his ale. The Devil, who was ever battling for St. Dunstan's soul, saw his chance. He offered to blight the orchards with frost and ruin the apple crop. Wily Dunstan accepted on the condition that the Old Chap did his worst on the 17th, 18th or 19th of May. Since then, if a frost falls on those days, St. Dunstan is blamed. Hence the saying: 'Tis a fight twixt the Devil and the maltster'.

Perhaps indicating that each year Dunstan is tempted, and if the frost comes, he's given in.

St. Dunstan's Day is May 19th, and it is exceedingly unlucky to make cider on that day.

Apples remaining on the trees after St. Dunstan's Day are said to be safe from blight and decay.

Devon too has rich vats of cider lore, and the men of Devon give a different version of the tale. The three days, 19th, 20th and 21st are known as St. Frankin's Days or 'Francemas'. There is, of course, no Saint in the annals of the Church of England named St. Frankin. It is a petname for Old Nick himself. Apparently the North Devon brewers made a blood pact with his Lordship, to the effect, that if they diluted their beer with unpleasant substances, he would send frosts to blight the apple blow and spoil the cider.

So if the frosts come in May, we know what's going on in Devon. Don't drink their beer!

Another version of the tale, states that Frankin was an Exeter brewer, who was so distressed by the ill effects of the cider trade on his business, that he bartered his soul for three nights of frost a year.

The terrible uncertainty of these three days are expressed in a Somerset saying:

'Till Culmstock Fair be come and gone,
There mid be apples or mid be none.'

Culmstock Fair was held on the 21st of May.

If an apple tree blossoms twice in one year a death in the family will follow.

It is also unlucky to have both fruit and blossom on the same tree. Remove the buds to avoid bereavement.

The haze of blossom and foliage often obscures the growing apples. Only when the blossom falls can the fruit be seen. This gives rise to the saying:

'The little apples be gone away vor sheep-shearing - and 'ont be back 'till harvest.'

Apple varieties are propagated by grafting. It is in spring that grafts of the desired variety are inserted under the bark of the crab or wilding rootstock.

To protect the graft it is covered with 'lute', clay mixed with fresh horse dung. This brew is known as 'cat' in Somerset. If the graft was onto a small stock, hot wax would be heated in a tiny cauldron and used instead.

The saddle graft, in which the grafting branch is joined to the top of the stock, was preferred in Somerset. The unique Somerset saddle graft was used. The stock tree, called a 'stem' or 'framework' tree, was allowed to develop ten or so good sturdy limbs. The limbs were all cut off back to the stock, and then a stick of the desired variety, known as the 'scion', was inserted under the bark of each, and a flap cut from its side, pulled over the stump and fixed across the top. The grafts would unite with the stock and grow a new framework of branches.

This type of headgraft has been favoured since mediaeval times. Traditionally standard trees were produced. The stocks had trunks 4-6 feet high, and their fruit-bearing branches towered into the sky. Modern orchardists tend to grow bush trees. These have shorter trunks, to make harvesting easier.

Like all propagation work, grafting is traditionally best carried out between the New Moon and the Full.

The grafters were often professionals, who passed their secrets down exclusively within their families.

Poet John Philips, included in his poem 'Cyder', the very old tradition that blackthorn stocks could have apple-bearing branches grafted onto them, and so produce hybrid fruit. Perhaps these 'apple-sloes' make cider with a sloe gin taste!

Query start here needs time

Midsummer Day (24th June) - Michaelmas (29th September)

Midsummer Eve was a time of enchantment, when the faerie world drew nearer. A piece of wicken would be carried for luck, and to protect against the pranks of pixies. 'Wicken' is an old Somerset name for the rowan tree.

Midsummer was also the best time for propagating apple trees by budding. A bud is taken from the desired parent, and inserted under the bark of a two year old rootstock within 6 inches of the ground. The apples this tree produces will have the qualities of the tree from which the bud was taken. In modern times, some favour this method over grafting.

Budding is best done after the New Moon and before the Full.

St. Swithin's Day is July 15th, and if it is raining on that day, it is said that, 'St. Swithin is christening the apples'.

July 25th was the day on which the apple trees were blessed by priests. Salisbury Cathedral preserves a service for this occasion.

There is one celebration which, in Somerset at least would not be the same without liberal servings of cider, the Harvest Home. To ease the burden of heavy work under a blistering sun, harvesters were granted unlimited helpings of the amber nectar.

When the corn was safely in the ricks, the Harvest Supper was held. The farmer supplied the fayre, which was eaten out of doors or in an ancient barn at trellis tables, with folk music, dance and song.

Today in Somerset, many parishes still hold their Harvest Supper. Here is motto spotted on a banner, hung on the wall at the East Brent Harvest Home in 1933:

'Beef and pudding, cheese and cider,
Are wont to make the waistcoat wider,
But let pudding and cider, cheese and beef,
Be the rich man's alms, the poor's relief.
With cheese and cider, beef and pudding,

Let no ill thought be found intruding.
And for pudding, cider, beef and cheese
Give thanks to Him who made us these.'

Apples are traditionally the first fruits offered at the Harvest Home.

The apple harvest, known as 'Apple-time', starts in earnest mid-September, and goes on sometimes into December. The different varieties of apple ripening at varying times.

Livestock are grazed in the orchard for nine months of the year. An old saying advises:

'Hain-up come Priddy Fair Day.'

Priddy Fair is held in the third week of August. This was the time to clear the orchard of livestock and cut the grass in preparation for Apple-time.

It is vital to remember only to pick apples when the moon is waning. If the moon is waxing, the apples are full and will not keep.

Normally the apples were left to fall naturally when ripe and were picked from the ground. Alternatively the fruits were poled down. The harvesters used long ash poles surmounted by an iron hook for shaking stubborn fruit from high branches. John Billingsley, writing in 1795, blamed poling for destroying the new buds and leaving the apple trees only able to bear fruit every two years.

Another method was to spread a sheet round a tree and shake it.

Wasps, known in Somerset as 'apple-drames', love ripe fruit, and can often be a problem at Apple-time. In 1706, John Philips suggested trapping them in treacle. He also regarded snails as avid orchard pests.

It is traditional, and almost blasphemous not to leave the small apples on the trees after harvest. These small apples are the property of the pixies, an offering of thanks for a bounteous crop. Boys will be boys though, and stealing these little apples was known as 'pixying' or 'pisking' in West Somerset, 'pixy-wording' or 'pixy-hoarding' on the Blackdowns, 'cull-pixying' in South Somerset, and 'griggling'in the East. 'Grig' is another word for pixy, 'He were so merry as a grig'.

The tradition of leaving the 'little apples', dates at least to classical Rome and is witnessed by the poet Virgil:

'Ah Amaryllis, now I know why you were putting up such wistful prayers and for whose sake you left the little apples hanging on the trees!'

(*The Dispossessed*, from the *Pastoral Poems*, E. V. Rieu's trans.)

In this poem the unharvested apples are left as an offering to the goddess Venus, to whom they are sacred, to win her favour and gain her help in making a love spell successful.

In former times a Somerset man might back up an opinion by exclaiming, 'As sure as God made little apples'.

The apples were collected into a 'picker' basket. These hold a 'peck', or twenty pounds of apples. These pickers were emptied into larger two-handled baskets named 'wooley butts', 'quarter sacks' or 'maunds'. These held three pecks, 50-60 pounds. All the picking baskets were made of withies.

It was rare for cider apples to be milled straight after harvesting. Sometimes they were left in the orchard piled into pyramidical tumps, covered with straw and allowed to 'come' for three or four weeks before milling.

The common practise in Somerset was for the apples to be taken up to the tallet or apple loft above the cider house, and lay there for a few weeks, protected by clean, dry straw.

The fruit was allowed to 'come' as this produced better cider. It allows the apples to lose some of their moisture and concentrates the sugars in the juice. A general mellowing takes place.

The apples were considered ready for milling when the cidermaker could easily make a dent in the skin with his fingernail.

Apple harvest was an appropriate time for procuring barrels to make the cider in. Oak was favourite but chestnut was also popular. Casks that had previously contained spirits were considered best, as they imparted flavour to the cider. Rum was top choice, with port and brandy coming close.

Casks holding one hoggshead or 54 gallons were favoured but other sizes such as the 120 gallon port pipe were used.

In the days of smuggling, many an empty rum cask was granted to farmers on outlying farms. Often as a reward for concealing contraband from the excisemen.

Before the days of sterilisation by campden tablet, it was important to blow into the bung hole of a cask to see if all was clean and sweet.

The lees or remnants of old cider was scrubbed from previously used casks, or removed by turning a chain around the inside. Scorching the walls with burning straw was another method.

Once Apple-time is over, the trees can be pruned, and live-stock can be let into the orchards to graze contentedly for another nine months.

Michaelmas (29th September) - Christmas Day (25th December)

Michaelmas was a time for fairs and jollity. Farms changed hands and labourers were hired. It was also the beginning of Allerntide, the Halloween season.

Maidens desiring to know which of their admirers would make the best husbands, went out 'Apple Grabbing'. gathering crab apples for divination. Somewhere safe, away from prying eyes, under the bed or in the attic, every girl laid out her crabs so that they formed the initials of each of her admirers.

Come Old Michaelmas Day, October 11th, these crab apple letters were carefully studied. Those unlucky men whose initials had rotted or fallen out of shape were discarded as lovers, while those whose monograms were fresh and comely were revealed to be good solid husband material.

Halloween, the evening of October 31st, was anciently considered the New Year, and as such was a prime time for divination, especially as it was believed to be a twilight time between the two primal seasons, summer and winter, when the gods, ancestral spirits and faery hosts had free reign.

These ancient beliefs were reflected by Church celebrations. November 1st was All Saints' Day. A service was held in remembrance of all the Church's holy ones, and November 2nd was All Souls' Day, when in the Roman Catholic Church, prayers were said for the departed.

At Allerntide excess stock was slaughtered to ensure enough Winter feed for breeding animals. This meant a time of festive plenty. Apples were in season, and as the cidermaking was in progress or about to begin, the old cider needed to be finished up.

On Exmoor, children would black their faces and go begging for 'Allern apples'.

All Hallow's Eve was the night for traditional observances. A feast was held, with games and lashings of mischief. In Somerset it is referred to as 'Punkie Night', or the 'Old Night'. At Hinton St. George a Punkie King and Queen, normally children, are elected to lead the celebratory procession.

Everywhere, apple games are part of the fun, especially apple 'duking'. Apples are set afloat in a bowl, and gamesters, with their arms tied behind their backs try to capture them in their mouths. In a rougher game, an apple and a candle are placed at opposite ends of a stick suspended from the ceiling. It is spun and the celebrants have to catch the apple in their mouths, again with their arms secured, risking a hefty wack from the fruit, singed hair or a mouthful of wax. It is believed that both these pastimes once had a divinatory purpose.

A gentler game was played by the children. Previously each child would have selected an apple, known as an 'Allern Apple', and stored it with nuts until the Old Night. Then an elder would choose which apple was the finest, and its owner was granted a prize of prime nuts.

Another competition was the carving of the 'Apple-well'. An apple's skin had to be removed unbroken in a special way. It was extremely lucky to produce a perfect apple-well. As a divination afterwards the peel is thrown over the left shoulder. If it lands whole, marriage is forecast. If the diviner is especially blessed, the skin will form the beloved's initial, but if the peel breaks, then a life of celibacy is foretold. (More details on the apple-well can be seen in *Caer Sidhe vol II* by Michael Bayley, published by Capall Bann.)

The girls would often undertake other methods of ascertaining their marriage prospects. Each would eat an apple, and after cut the core and remove the pips. If a pip is severed by the knife, then the course of love will not run smooth. The pips are counted off to a rhyme which foretells the trade of the future spouse, 'Tinker, tailor, soldier, sailor, butcher, baker, candlestick maker, poorman, beggarman, thief'.

In another spell, each girl would choose an apple, tie it with string and suspend it from the mantle over the fire. The heat would cause the apples to fall into the flames, and the order in which they fell determined the order in which the girls would marry.

One final divination was done in private, again to see who Fate had set aside as a husband. To set the spell in motion, the inquiring girl would eat an apple in front of her looking glass, at midnight, alone in a darkened room. If she was lucky the face of her future husband would peer over her shoulder. If no one came, there would be no wedding that year, but if the Devil showed his face, she was his for eternity. If only white cloth was seen, it was her shroud and omened death. One unlucky girl was said to have spied a coffin with 'October 31st' written on it. She died of fright.

Apart from plentiful cider the traditional beverage of the Halloween season was 'lambswool'; a punch of hot ale and sugar, spiced with nutmeg, and graced by floating roast apples and pieces of toast.

The name lambswool originates from the Gaelic 'La Mas Ubhal', pronounced 'lamasu'l', which means 'The Day of Apple Fruit', an old title for the 1st of November. In legend this day is sacred to the angel presiding over fruit and seeds.

One Somerset folksong associated with the Halloween season was 'Holly Boy and Ivy Girl', alternatively known as 'Green Ivy O'. The third verse sings of apples:

'O the ivy O, at the Allern tide
And the holly he is yellow
There be apples fell adown and they picks 'n from the ground
And they lays 'n in the tallat side to side
O 'tis ivy O, green ivy O
O the ivy at Allern tide.'

The tune was originally for pipe and tabor, and the song would have been performed as a processional dance.

The festivities of Halloween over, the serious business is begun.

Traditionally cidermaking should start on All Saints' Day, November 1st. Some begin it earlier, but in no circumstances should it start on a Friday. There is also a tradition that fishermen should not sail on a Friday. These beliefs are memories of Friday as the pagan day of rest. Latterly it was regarded as the sabbath of faeries and witches.

The first job of cidermaking is to mill the apples, to crush them ready for the juice to be extracted. The earliest cidermakers would have crushed their apples by hand, rolling a stone wheel on them in a trough, or by pounding them with long handled wooden pestles.

These methods were superseded by the horsepowered circular stone mill. Normally an older, less-than-frisky horse was chosen.

The apples are stirred down from the apple-tallet above into a circular stone trough. Around this the horse walks pulling a huge stone wheel over the apples. A hundredweight of fruit is pressed at a time. The cidermaker walks behind the horse ensuring the mill is not clogged by pulp.

No farmer would admit to adding water to cider. It is sacrilegious, the purer the cider the better, but at this stage some would throw in one or two buckets to stop the pulp becoming too thick. The pulp begins to oxidise turning a rich brown. If, when squeezed in the hand, it retains its shape, it is well milled.

John Worlidge invented the 'Ingenio', a rotary or scratter mill, and published his design in his *Vinetum Brittanicum* of 1678. The Ingenio was worked by hand, the apples being crushed between a toothed roller and a fixed comb. It was based on a Cuban sugar mill.

Mills derived from this design soon became conspicuous. The pulp was not as fine as that produced on a circular stone mill, but the speed of production was far greater. Rotary mills were capable of milling several tons of apples per hour, whereas circular stone mills were limited to three hundredweight per half-hour.

Traditionalists were slow to change to rotary mills as they did not crush the pips. 'Gribbles' impart aromatic oils and a fine bitter 'woody' taste.

Leaves and twigs are separated from the fruit before milling, but no one would dream of washing it. This may be a practical belief as no yeast is added to produce fermentation in cider. Natural yeasts from the orchard may find their way in on the appleskins.

Secret practices are rife even at this stage of cidermaking. In Ireland quinces are thrown in for 'sharpness'. Another very old way is to add crab apples to achieve that special 'bite'. It is also believed that a few rotten apples help to clarify the cider.

It is considered 'cheeky', but to get a good rich colour, some have been known to add elderberries, blackberries, or even beetroot.

Apples, once milled are known as 'pummy', or more properly 'pomace'.

The second job of cidermaking is to press the fruit. The cider press, along with the mill, was a vital and much cherished piece of machinery.

In Somerset today, many farms have an old mill or press tucked away in a barn, and even if they don't make cider anymore, these family heirlooms are kept, 'just for luck'.

The most common type of press in Somerset was triple screwed, with the two outer screws worked by gears from the central one. Originally the screws were wooden, but by the end of the eighteenth century most had been replaced by iron. Designs varied and often the village blacksmith created or repaired cider machinery to the farmer's individual specifications. These presses were operated by hand.

Before pressing it is traditional to leave the pummy exposed to the air for up to two days. This brings out the flavour. Lavoisier recommends spreading the pummy out and exposing it for 24 hours, turning it once or twice. This process is known as maceration. The 'pummy' oxidises, turning a deep brown colour, and fermentation begins, increasing the pectin and pectase content.

The pummy is carried to the press in wooden shovels. All cider equipment is by necessity of wood. Metal would be dissolved by the cider's acids. Everything is scrubbed thoroughly clean before use.

Milled apples are notoriously slippery and difficult to handle. The various cider counties developed ways to overcome this. In Somerset a 'cheese' was built. Combed wheat or barley straw was used. This straw had to be clean and sweet. Some preferred barley straw as it imparted a richer colour to the cider.

The bed of the press is covered by straw, carefully placed, first north-south, then east-west. A layer of pummy is spread on top. Then comes the second layer of straw. Pummy and straw are alternated, building up to twelve layers. The 'cheese' is pyramidal to give strength, with the ends of the straw protruding.

Another way is to build the cheese in a square frame. The straw ends are folded over and pushed into the pummy. The square is removed before pressing. Hazel spars are used to hold it in place while the next layer is built. A cheese built like this should be straight sided. Each cheese layer is tapped until it is flat, with an 'apple pounder'.

A heavy board is laid across the cheese to spread the force applied by the press. This is referred to as a 'vollyer' or 'hatch'.

After cheesebuilding, most cidermakers would leave the cheese overnight before pressing. The cider takes a better colour from apples left to stand, and a new cheese is prone to split under pressure.

Only the slightest load should be put on the cheese as pressing starts or a flood may result. Tradition has it that the youngest person present should be first to sample the fresh juice, sucking it up through a natural straw.

The pressed juice runs into a stone trough.

When the sides of the cheese protrude under pressure, they are scraped off with a hay knife or preferably, a special tool known as a 'cheese cutter', and piled on top. The cheese may be pressed in a night or gradually over a whole week, between farm chores.

An old-style cidermaker would simply transfer the fresh juice from the press trough into wooden pails with a 'dipper', carry it to his casks, and pour it in through a wooden funnel known as a 'tundish' or 'tunnacre'. Then leave it to ferment, relying entirely on nature.

The cheese, devoid of juice and a quarter its original size was taken outside to the pasture, and fed to the cows. The stock loved it so much that often it would have to be left in several heaps to avoid them quarrelling. Another use was as fertiliser for sickly apple trees. Old pomace was bad for stock as it would ferment, and become strong enough to intoxicate the heaviest bull.

With the cider safely in the butts the most crucial time begins. A slow fermentation ensures a good cider, a hasty one can cause problems. Low temperatures keep the fermentation steady. The cool cider cellars help but what is really needed is a good frost. Otherwise a cidermaker has to constantly listen at his casks, and if he hears too much 'mirth', or rapid fermentation, then there is nothing for it but to rack off the cider into a fresh cask. Fermentation then has to start again.

For the first few weeks the cask is not sealed, but allowed to froth freely from the bunghole as the natural sugars are fermented. It is essential to top the cider up each day with juice as air must not be allowed to mix in. Once the fermentation has settled to a gentle hissing, the cask is bunged down, gently at first, but then securely, and sometimes sealed with lime cement.

Over the next months, a second fermentation takes place. The yeasts mellowing the tannins and acids.

Another problem is cider that will not start to ferment. This is referred to as 'sullen'. The oldest remedy is to thrust a handful of orchard earth into the cask. Lumps of meat and strips of rabbit skin have also proved successful.

Here we get onto the contentious subject of 'additives'. Legends suggest that all sorts of things were dropped into the casks. Cider is highly acid and will 'eat' anything. Meat was often introduced to give 'body', a leg of mutton, side of pork or beef, even hooves. Some scurrilously suggest that cider that has not had a rat dissolved in it, is markedly inferior. Wheat and barley also give body. Sugar, boiled black was used to give colour, but was generally frowned upon.

The most unusual of the 'secret' practises at this stage was 'Toad Swimming', and I have spoken with a Cornishman who actually remembers it being done. Before the cask was bunged down a good fat live toad was added to 'work' the cider. The toad would swim around dreaming blissful amber dreams, 'cleaning' the cider as it passed through his body.

Apparently cider-toads could live up to twenty years. When the cask was finally emptied, the toad would be tipped through the bung, caught, and kept for his next 'swim'. In Mr. Bath's novel *'Uncle Kit's Legacy'*, Siah Penpol was described as an old fashioned sort, who always put a toad into a cider cask to 'work it'.

'Mind the toad, mind the toad, save 'un up for the next brewen!'

The cider can be ready in 6-8 weeks, but is often best after April. In a cold winter the fermentation can become dormant and restart with the spring.

Good cider properly made and sealed can keep for many years, increasing in virtue and strength.

Each cidermaker developed his own methods. Sweeter ciders were produced by many rackings, or naturally by selecting sweeter apple varieties.

John Billingsley in 1795 gave details of the fermentation process, dividing it into three. The first fermentation he named 'vinous'. This takes 2-3 days for sharper apples, 7-10 for sweeter, and converts the 'must' into a transparent spiritous liquor. The second fermentation, 'acetous' turns the cider to vinegar, and the third 'putrefactive' disengages alkali from the liquor. Both the second and third are to be avoided. After or just before the vinous fermentation ends, the casks are 'strummed'. Sulphur matches are ignited inside the cask to kill the yeast and cease further fermentation.

The cider is racked into an open vessel and left for a day, then barrelled and stored for use.

For sweeter cider he recommends 'kieving', a method which involves starting the fermentation in an open vessel. A brown head forms. When this cracks, revealing white froth level with the surface of the head, a cask should be prepared by pouring in 15 gallons and then 'strumming'. The rest of the cider is now added and left to mature until February, then it is racked off. The cask is strummed again, the cider put back in, and the cask sealed until required.

A poor quality cider was sometimes produced for giving to less deserving servants and vagrants. The pressed pomace was soaked in water, repressed and the resulting liquid put in a cask. It fermented into a thin liquor known as 'ciderkins'.

Christmas Day (25th December) - Lady Day (25th March)

The Twelve Days of Christmas were of course avidly celebrated and involved liberal cider consumption. The festive season was extended by the remembrance of the eleven days lost in the calendar change of 1752.

It was considered unlucky to work on Old Christmas Day. In a time when no statuary holidays were received apart from village revels and fairs, a lengthy rest from labour was much appreciated. The year's end was the only time when the demands of agriculture and husbandry allowed an extended break.

Anticipation of Christmas Eve and the start of the season is expressed in the Somerset dialect 'Farm Labourers Carol':

'Kirs'mas Eve ool zoon be he-ar
This ool be my desire
A piece of burd and raw milk cheese
And a jolly good cup of zider'.

Christmas Eve was traditionally celebrated at night by a gathering of family and friends around the vast open hearth. Somerset knew the old custom of the Yule log, as well as a more local variant, 'The Burning of the Ashen Faggot'.

The Yule log custom has survived, but in the days of wide hearths, the log would have measured five feet or more in length.

On Christmas Eve while still light, the men would leave the house armed with axes. A good strong log was cut, either oak, anciently sacred to Thor, to protect against thunder, or apple, Baldur's wood, to attract good luck.

The men would elect one of their number as the 'King of Yule'. He would ride the log's back as it was dragged by strong ropes, all the way back to the house.

The rest of the household endeavoured to dislodge the 'Yule King'. If he reached the farm still mounted it was a cause for much celebration as he brought good luck in with him. He was rewarded with lambswool and cakes.

The Yule log was ceremoniously placed in the hearth and kindled with a brand carefully saved from last year's log. It would burn throughout the whole twelve days of Christmas.

The Ashen Faggot is peculiar to the West Country, particularly Somerset. It was a bundle of ash twigs often seven or eight feet long, sometimes twisted resembling a figure eight, and bound with withies, either nine or as many as possible. It could weigh a hundredweight.

The ceremony always took place in good company, often in a public house.

The Faggot was placed on the fire. In the heat, the withy bands would snap loudly. As each one went those assembled would take another tot of either cider or 'egg-hot', a mix of cider and eggs.

The Faggot was also used for divination. The youngsters present would each select a withy as their own. The order in which they snapped determined the order in which they would marry.

The ash tree is sacred to Woden, and willow is regarded as a tree of divination, through its association with the moon goddess, and anciently, Isis of Egypt.

The Ashen Faggot is still burnt at the King William IV at Curry Rivel, where a secret wish is made every time a withy snaps, and at the Luttrell Arms, Dunster, where it is believed that the faggot commemorates the one burnt to warm St. Mary and her child.

When the ceremony of wassailing the apple trees is done on Christmas Eve, the two are combined and the ashen faggot burnt first.

The last unburnt ash stick from the faggot is kept in the byre to safeguard calving cattle, and used to kindle the next year's faggot.

The traditional fayre for Christmas Day was roast beef with crab apple jelly, washed down with plenty of best cider, while the better off followed the ancient Germanic custom of feasting on boar's head, complete with apple in mouth.

Cidermakers are wont to say, 'Hot Summers and cold Winters be the makin' o' good cider', and consider that the trees must be well covered with snow to produce an ample harvest.

Another belief was that the sun must shine through the trees on Christmas Day to ensure a good crop,

On a gloomier note it was also said that if blossom formed in December, one of the family would die in January.

There are many accounts of the ceremony of 'wassailing the apple trees'. It is the festive highlight of the cidermakers' year. No almanac would be complete without it.

The term 'wassail', originated in the Saxon toast, 'Waes-heal', literally, 'Be in health'.

The wassail takes two distinct forms, both of which have evolved from the same practice. The first is referred to as the 'visiting wassail'. It takes place on any night or number of nights from Christmas Eve on. A party of revellers, often dressed oddly, perhaps with their faces blacked, make a round of their neighbours. With them they carry an ash or apple vessel, known as the 'wassail bowl'. This is brimming with lambswool or cider punch. Varying wassail songs are sung, which always include a verse begging for donations of drink, cakes or money. In some counties the wassailers elect a 'Captain' or 'King' to keep them in line.

The visiting wassail takes place in Drayton and Curry Rivel on Old Christmas Eve, January 5th, and is remembered in Langport, where the following song was sung:

'Wassail, wassail all over the town;
Your cup it is white, and your beer it is brown;
Your bowl it is made of the good ashen tree;
And your beer is brewed of the best barley;
Langport bull-dog have lost his big tail
In the night that we go, a-singing wassail.'

Chorus:

'The Black Dog of Langport have a-burned off his tail;
And this is the night of our jolly wassail;
Vor tis our wassail,
And tis your wassail,
And joy be to you, vor tis our wassail.'

Another version was recorded at Barrington near Ilminster.

It is possible that this custom preserves the pagan original of carol singers traversing from door to door, performing for treats or charity.

In the Cotswolds the wassail bowl was decorated with evergreens and small dolls.

The Exmoor and Brendon Hills tradition of the 'Holly Riders' is stranger still. Groups of mounted men swinging lanterns and sporting holly sprigs on their clothes and wreaths round their hats, rode from farm to farm singing carols in return for cider, cakes or pennies.

The second form of the wassail is the serenading of the apple trees, epitomised by the ceremony which still takes place at Carhampton on the West Somerset coast. Dates for the service vary from district to district, but most accept Old Twelfth Night, January 17th, as the correct tide. A fitting marker to see out the last day of the old festive season.

The Old Twelfth Night date agrees with ancient practise. The Saxon tribes measured time by a bound lunar calendar of twelve and sometimes thirteen lunar months. All their religious feasts were movable, and chiefly held at Full or New Moons. The two lunar months either side of the Winter Solstice were named 'Yule'. The actual feast of 'Yule' was held at the Full Moon nearest the Winter Solstice. For this twelve days of rest were taken, and in a thirteen month year, thirteen. Each day represented a month of the coming year, omens as to its auspiciousness being taken from the events of that day.

As Yule was a Full Moon, their Twelfth Night would be just before a New Moon. An apt time to celebrate the ancient wassail.

The Carhampton wassail takes place in the orchard behind the Butcher's Arms on the evening of January 17th. Old accounts of the festivities tell how the Master of Ceremonies would carry an oaken bucket filled with cider out to the chosen tree. The crowd followed him and encircled the tree, armed with lanterns, shotguns and accordions. The Master then called for the singing of the Wassail Song:

'Old apple tree we wassail thee,

And hoping thou would bear,

For the Lord doth know where we shall be,

Till apples come another year,

For to bear well and to bloom well,

So merry let us be,

Let ev'ry man take off his hat

And shout out to the old apple tree:'

Chorus (shouted):

'Old Apple Tree we wassail thee

And hoping thou would bear

Hatsful, capsful, three bushel bagsful

And a little heap under the stairs

Hip hip hooray,

Hip hip hooray,

Hip hip, hooray.'

As the last cheer went up, the guns were discharged through the branches into the night.

The Master would then place an offering of toast soaked in cider, in a fork of the tree. Straight away, the accordions would start up with folksongs such as *'The Little Brown Jug'*. *'The Barley Mow'*, and *'Blackbird'*. The hot cider was drunk, and as soon as it was finished the company would adjourn to the pub to carry on the good cheer.

A similar wassail song was collected by the famed folksong scholar Cecil Sharp at Bratton.

Although a few public wassails take place in Somerset, most are private family occasions held in the smaller orchards.

The most publicised event is that sponsored by the Taunton Cider Company. It takes place at Norton Fitzwarren and features a new innovation in the form of a pretty young 'Wassail Queen', who makes the traditional offering.

The wassail survived at Molland until 1870. Milverton was recorded as holding one in 1904, and the Walton Wassail was held at the Globe until 1969, when the pub changed hands becoming the Pike and Musket.

From recorded details and folk-memory let us reconstruct what a traditional Somerset wassail would have been like two or three hundred years ago.

Farmers, labourers, friends and family gathered in the farmhouse. The food had been in preparation all day and spirits were high. The last of the old cider was to be used up.

The most respected elder was chosen as Master of Ceremonies, and at the appointed time he rose and led the company out to the orchard. In centuries past, wassailing was a male preserve, and the women would wait in the farmhouse.

The orchard would have been prepared that day. A bonfire blazed at the entrance, welcoming and warming. In the topmost branches, carved mangold lanterns perched, casting flickering light.

The wassailers would carry sticks, clubs, hunting horns, tin pots, pans, a basket of apples and a milk pail of cider with toast and roasted apples floating on top. The Master would bear a large two or three handled wassail cup, or an ancient drinking horn brimming with hot cider, enlivened by ginger and gin.

They would gather around the most venerable tree, the seat of the Orchard spirit, the Apple Tree Man or Lazy Lawrence. It is this spirit, representative of all the trees, whose health is drunk and to whom the offerings are made in remembrance of the last apple harvest, and as an appeal for a bumper crop in the coming year.

The Master calls for the Wassail Song.

This version was recorded in the neighbourhood of Wellington and has the same roots as the visiting wassail songs. Similar words are recorded as being sung at an orchard wassail in Winchcombe:

'Wassail, wassail, all round our town,
Our cup it is white, our ale it is brown.
Our bowl is made of the good old ash tree,
So now my brave fellows, lets drink unto thee,

Chorus:

'Hatsfuls, capsfuls, dree bushel bagfuls'
And a gurt heap under the stairs.
Hip, Hip, Hurrah!

There was an old man who had an old cow,
And for how to keep her, he couldn't tell how,
So he built up a barn for to keep his cow warm,
And a little more cider won't do us no harm.

Chorus

Harm, me boys, harm; harm, me boys, harm.
A little more cider won't do us no harm.

Chorus

Down in an old lane there lived an old fox,
And all day long he sat mopping his chops,
Shall we go and catch him, oh yes, if we can,
Ten thousand to one if we catch him or not,

Chorus

Harm, me boys, harm; harm, me boys, harm.
A little more cider won't do us no harm.

A poor little robin sits up in the tree,
And all the day long so merry sings he,
A-widdling and twiddling to keep himself warm,
And a little more cider won't do us no harm,

Chorus

Harm, me boys, harm; harm, me boys, harm.
A little more cider won't do us no harm.

A lady comes round with her silver pin,
Pray open the door and let us all in,
For this is our 'sail, our jolly wassail,
And jolly go we to our jolly wassail.

Chorus

Harm, me boys, harm; harm, me boys, harm.
A little more cider won't do us no harm.
Hip, Hip, Hurrah!'

With the cheers as much noise as possible is made. Horns are blown, the pots banged and rattled, and the staves beaten on the trunk of the tree. Before the advent of firearms it is probable that arrows were fired through the branches.

Next the offerings are made. Cider-soaked cakes are placed in the branches, and a libation of cider and roast apples poured over the roots. The wassailers themselves take a hearty swig.

The ritual is that of a communion meal. The celebrants eat and drink of the blood and body of the apple-spirit, and offer itself to itself, a religious practise common among the Teutonic peoples, and mirrored in the Norse Elder Edda, in the poem *'Lay of the High One'*. The god Odin, the Saxon Woden, is:

'Pierced by a spear, pledged to Odin, Offered, myself to myself.'

(*Norse Poems*, W.H. Auden and Paul B. Taylor)

Countrymen have said that the noise and threatening behaviour is to frighten away evil spirits who may blight the crop. Folklorist Ralph Whitlock suggested the hullaballoo was to wake the slumbering tree spirit. Another explanation can be sought in Teutonic legend, as the wassail ceremony, like its name, probably takes its modern form from Saxon culture. The noise making is a ritual enactment of the myth of the god Baldur.

James Rendel Harris in his book *'The Origin and Meaning of Apple Cults'*, derives the name Baldur from the same primitive root as 'apple-tree', 'ap·l-dur', and considers him an apple-god.

The worshippers of Baldur left his name on the English landscape; Balderwood in the New Forest, Balderstone in Lancashire, Balderton in both Cheshire and Notts, as well as at Appledore in Devon.

Baldur was known as 'the beautiful', and was regarded as kind god, a bringer of joy. That he was an apple and cider deity is not so strange when it is considered that all the gods had tree personifications, Woden was the ash, Thor the oak. Even in the great classical mystery cults of Greece and Rome, Dionysus and Bacchus were venerated as gods of the vine and the vintage.

The Saxons worshipped the same pantheon as the Norse peoples, but left less literary remains. So we turn to the Norse Eddas for Baldur's story.

The god Baldur, son of Woden and Frigga was loved by all the gods, but Frigga, his mother had been worried by a premonition of his doom. She set out to safeguard his life, by seeing that all creation, fire, water, iron, all the animals, the birds, poisons, and snakes, swore never to touch a hair of his head. However, she overlooked one plant because it was too young, and seemed so insignificant, the mistletoe.

Once the gods knew nothing could harm Baldur, they made a game out of trying to injure him. Gracefully he let them have their fun. All took turns in casting weapons at him. None had any effect.

Loki, the mischief maker, fashioned an arrow of mistletoe and waited his chance. Loki is a mysterious figure, sometimes he is a friend to the gods, and at other times a deadly enemy. Some see in him a reflection of Lucifer, but he is better perceived as a personification of the dark side of nature, the shadow of cunning and envy that runs through humanity, and the gods.

Hödur, Baldur's blind brother stood alone, listening to the fun and games, unable to join in. Loki offered his aid and lent Hödur his bow. He strung the mistletoe arrow and guided Hödur, who sent it flying straight into Baldur's heart.

So Hödur slew his beloved brother.

The wassailers echo this dangerous game, pretending to harm the tree, and then making offerings to amend the crime. Many authorities quote old wassailers as saying, 'The toast is for the robins', and at Torquay in Devon a small boy was hoisted into the branches to play the bird's part, crying, 'Tit, tit, more to eat'.

The robin in folklore is considered sacred:

'The robin and the wren are God's cock and hen'.

The robin's red breast associates him with blood and sacrifice. This memory is preserved in the legend that the robin's breast was stained red when the compassionate bird plucked a thorn from Christ's crown as he made his way to Calvary. Perhaps the story was transferred from Baldur to the new sacrificed god, Jesus Christ.

Baldur is, like Jesus, reborn with the spring. In winter the apple trees are bare, because Balder is in the underworld awaiting rebirth.

Wassailers in Yorkshire were at one time known to carry a figure of Christ on the cross. The image of the crucified Christ strangely echoes the pagan image of a beautiful young god tied to a tree and pierced with an arrow. Reminiscent of this is St. Sebastian, martyred by a shower of arrows and a beating with clubs. His feast day, the anniversary of his death, falls on the 20th January.

After the offering the wassailers move on to the next tree. They wassailed all those trees that bore well, until the cider ran dry. Then they trudged back to the farmhouse where more drink and food awaited them.

The women would have carefully bolted the doors locking their men out. The wassailers were only let in when one of them guessed correctly what treat was cooking on the spit. The lucky guesser received the special fayre all to himself. If this ritual was neglected, or if any of the family were absent the whole wassail was jeopardised and the trees would not bear.

Inside, the hot cider and songs continued, with dancing to the fiddle and bass viol. If the wassailers were smallholders they would later proceed to the next orchard and repeat the performance. In isolated districts the same men would travel on different nights to wassail outlying orchards. This is recorded in South and West Somerset. In the Minehead district up to twenty orchards would be visited in a night. Some wassailers would end up considerably drunk, and a few have been spotted wassailing Mulberry bushes on the way home.

The orchards of unpopular men would be missed out as a curse. An orchard that is not wassailed cannot be expected to produce.

Literary references to the wassail in Somerset, date back to John Aubrey's 'Remains of Gentilisme', 1686:

'... So in Somersetshire when the wassaile (which is on.... I think Twelve-Eve) the Ploughmen have their Twelve-cake, and they go into the Ox-house to the Oxen, with the Wassell-bowl and drink to the ox with crumpled horn, that treads out the corne ; they have an old concerved rhythme; and afterwards they goe with their Wassel-bowle into the orchard and goe about the trees to blesse them, and putt a piece of tost upon the roots in order to it.'

The wassailing of the oxen appears in John Brand's *'Observations on Popular Antiquities'*, 1900, and records the practise in Herefordshire. There each ox is called by name and toasted. That the oxen are included in the old ceremony is not a surprise. The ox was the ancient animal of the plough, the horse being adopted only recently. The cereal crop depended on these sturdy beasts, and like the apple trees they were celebrated in this way. For the twelve days of Christmas they too would be at rest, and on Christmas Eve it was believed they knelt in their stalls.

Brand also recalls the male wassailers being locked out of the house until they have sung 'well' enough for the females to relent and let them enter.

The Wellington wassail song contains memories of all these traditions. The second verse, the wassail of the oxen, the fourth, the offering to the robin, and the fifth, the lady of the house letting the men in to the festivities, opening the door with her 'silver pin'.

The 'silver pin' is perhaps a reminder of the symbolic key-shaped ornament that Saxon women wore on their belts. This showed that they ruled inside the home, while the men ruled out in the world. Times have changed!

Another old Herefordshire tradition recorded by Brand has Somerset echoes:

'The farmers with their friends and servants meet together, and about six o'clock walk out to a field where wheat is growing. In the highest part of the ground twelve small fires and one large one are lighted up. The attendants, headed by the master of the family, pledge the company in old cider, which circulates freely .... A circle is formed around the large fire, when a general shout and hallooing takes place, which

you hear answered from all the adjacent villages and fields. Sometimes fifty or sixty of these fires may all be seen at once.'

In her *'Somerset Folklore'*, Ruth Tongue writes of thirteen fires lit at about this season to burn the vegetable rubbish collected hedging and ditching. One fire is larger than the others to represent Jesus Christ. The twelve are his disciples. One of these is set apart from the rest and built of the worst rubbish. This burns slow and symbolises Judas Iscariot.

Bale fires built on hills are another remnant of pagan festivals. The council of the Aesir, the Teutonic gods numbered thirteen. A large fire was burned for Woden the Chief, eleven lesser for his compatriots, and the thirteenth for Loki the trickster.

Until recently red-headed people were regarded as unlucky in Somerset. An old countryman told me that during 'First Footing' at New Year, when a dark-haired man brings bread, salt and coal into the house, no red-head was allowed to be inside.

This has been explained as a hereditary aversion to the red-headed invader Danes, or to the tradition that Judas was a red-headed man. Loki was traditionally a red-head too, and his animal form was the fox, with whom he shared familiar attributes: cunning and thievery. After he caused Balder's death, the Aesir hunted him down. Perhaps he is the fox in the third verse of the wassail song.

'There was an old fox down in a green copse. Clothing his den and smacking his chops;'

(wassail song variant)

On a lighter note, if you hold a wassail, here is an essential recipe for wassail punch, 'borrowed' from Ralph Whitlock's *'Calendar of Country Customs'*.

(For 12 persons)

5 quarts of dry cider

1 teaspoon grated nutmeg

7 tablespoons of brown sugar

2 bananas (sliced fresh before serving)

3 sliced oranges

1 teaspoon grated cinnamon

4 cloves

Serve it hot!

To complete the cider cycle here's an old rhyme concerning the best time to plant trees. Candlemas is celebrated on February 2nd, and is the feast of 'First Lights', the first glimmer of springtime:

'Apples, pears, hawthorn, quicken, oak,
Set them at All Hallows Tide and command them to prosper;
Set them at Candlemas,
and intreat them to grow.'

And remember to plant only on the New Moon!

Appendix

Cider Stories

While I was researching this book, I met and talked to cider makers, cider drinkers, and numerous other folk who were just interested in cider, and had a tale or a memory to share. They entertained me with numerous stories and anecdotes. Some were funny, others informative, a few were poignant, and while they had no place in the text of this book, it seemed a shame not to share them with those who're interested.

As to whether the wilder tales are true or not - well they seemed true when they were passed on to me, and a rum story always goes down better with a little cider!

Drinking Tales

My Neighbour

My next door neighbour's a good old boy, and he's been drinking cider all his life, man and boy. Worked on the farms he did. Up at dawn, down with a quart, toil 'till lunch, drink more cider and eat, work some more, then home for a pint and a feed, then up the pub for a few pints more.

Anyway he's retired now, and I usually give him a lift to the pub at lunchtime where he has a pint or two of the rough. Then he's back there at night, putting back four, or maybe six pints, even more at the weekend.

He's sixty-four now, huffs and puffs like a billows, as bandy as a coot, and as red as an apple in the face. He don't look a day over eighty!

(Watchet)

The Inglenook

I remember years ago, when the old pubs had huge fireplaces as wide as a barn's door. There'd be a bread oven in one of the walls, and maybe a ham or two hanging, curing up the chimney, suspended from black iron hooks. There'd always be a raging log fire, kept in check by two iron fire dogs. Them old boys, the sorts that live in the pub from morning until closing, would actually sit inside the fireplace, all in a row on old wooden benches and stools, each clutching a walking stick and pewter tankard. Some of them would take four hours to down a mug of cider, while others would swallow eight or more glasses a night. In winter they'd get nearer and nearer the fire, their faces glowing redder and redder in the heat and flame light.

One night, when I was about twenty, everyone was hard at it, an' it was so cold outside we were heating up fire pokers to warm our cider. What you do, is wait until they glow red, then cool them by sticking them on one of the pub's oak beams. It used to singe the wood it did. The marks are still there. Then we'd poke them in our cider mugs. Sometimes the cider would bubble, but then it'd be nice and warming as it went down.

Anyhow, them old boys were all there, not really saying anything jus' musing and drinking, their eyes reflecting the fire. Every now an' then one of them would shuffle his stool nearer the flames. After a while, my mate Bill Vellows came in, and asked, 'What's cooking?' He said he could smell a joint roasting. We thought nothing of it. Then someone else said the same. In the end we could all smell it and I asked the landlord what was cooking, 'Nothing!' he replied.

We drank some more and thought no more of it. Then one of the old boys sitting in the fireplace started hollarin', 'Jim, Jim, wakey up my sport!' He was pulling at the man next to him, and then waving his fingers in the air as if he'd burnt them. I shot to my feet as soon as I realised what had happened. Old Jim at the end was roasting. He was sitting close to the fire, and he'd slipped away into heaven while we'd all bin' talking and laughing. As the fire had been built up and got fiercer, he'd got hotter and hotter.

Some of the lads lifted him out, and he was steaming like a joint taken out of the oven. Bright red he was and cooked into the one position, with his legs all bent and one hand clutching his tankard, just like he'd been sitting.

(told in a pub near Yeovil)

Hosiah's Wagon

This tale took place on the Somerset Levels just after the First War. I'm telling it to you, just as my father told it to me, and my grandfather, his father, told it to him.

Somerset was an old fashioned place then. Many farms still used horses to pull carts and plough, and most made their own cider. My grandfather was named Thomas, but was known to his old cronies as, 'Cider Tom', because it was his boast that he made the strongest cider north of Bridgwater.

New people were moving into the area, and the farm next to ours had been bought by an ex-military man, one Colonel Frederick Parkhurst, a rather old fashioned army type, but a good fellow for all that. One Sunday afternoon, he announced to Tom, that he was going to be entertaining a group of army pals the next weekend, explaining that as they'd all seen service at the front, there was nothing they liked more than having a drink and trying to make sense of it. Now, Tom took this as a challenge, 'Have you ever tried cider?'

'Can't say I have. Why?'

'Well, if you and your fellow officers think you can handle a drop or two, I'll have you over here for a sampling of my own cider. In fact, you can share my special cider, made just from the one old tree. That one over there.' He pointed it out.

The next Saturday night, it was cold, snow lay crisp and new on the ground, growing harder as the temperature plummeted further. The sky was black blue, silver stars gleaming like holes in a dark velvet curtain, drawn over a window on a sunny day. The officer duly arrived with three of his comrades, all decked in their military finest, their breath blowing in clouds as they trudged up the farm path.

Tom made them heartily welcome. There was Colonel Parkhurst, a young man Samuel Webster, a slightly rotund gentleman from the Irish Guards named Patrick O'Keefe, and the tall moustachioed Roger Galsworthy. As they shook hands in his doorway, the sound of horse's hooves riddled the air, and round the bend came a strong looking horse, born to the work of the farm. It was in harness to a battered old wooden farm wagon. Hunched over the reigns was a strange figure, seemingly headless, wrapped against the cold in a tattered cloak and several scraps of hessian sacking. The officers gaped at the weird apparition. The cart drew up right by them and a gnarled head appeared from the dusty cloak, its face red and lined with years and weather. Tom beamed, 'Hosiah!'

'Mr Tom', the driver addressed him respectfully in broad Somerset.

'Go into the kitchen and pour yourself a little something, Hosiah, to take the chill out of your bones.'

'Obliged.'

Tom turned from the cart and its driver, and motioned the men inside.

Colonel Parkhurst hesitated, 'If you don't mind me asking, who is that chap?'

'Oh, it's old Hosiah, he'll be running an errand for me later.'

The Colonel looked puzzled but didn't question further. Tom led them into the huge farmhouse parlour. Within an hour the two-handled cider mug had been round numerous times, and their faces were growing redder, their voices louder and laughter deeper.

The youngest of the officers, Samuel Webster passed the mug to his neighbour and spoke, 'Well, there doesn't seem to be much strength in this cider.'

His brother officers grimaced at his impropriety, but Tom just wryly smiled as he filled the old cider mug to overflowing again, from the barrel set in pride of place on the kitchen table.

As the mug came round to the younger man, Tom questioned him, 'Would you like something a little stronger perhaps?'

Trying to make up for his earlier remark Samuel smiled warmly, 'Not at all old chap, cider's fine. We are having a special cider drinking evening after all.'

Tom grinned, 'Well, you could all try drinking it like we farmers do.'

He produced a vast bottle of gin and topped up the cider mug with it, 'Half and half,' he explained.

They drank on, splicing Tom's special cider with his best gin, laughing in fine fettle. The hours sped by, and the health of everyone, including the king, was drunk with the best intentions.

Finally, after much congratulations and back slapping it was decided to break up the party.

At the farmhouse door, Tom was thanked again and again for a fine evening. Coat collars were turned up and hats adjusted. From inside, they could see that Hosiah had resumed his hunched position at the reigns of the cart. Young Samuel was the first to step out into the snow. He had taken four steps when he collapsed like he'd been shot, and lay prostrate, face down in the snow, overcome with cider and the below freezing temperature.

The chubby officer stepped out into the night, hurrying to help his comrade. He walked four yards, went suddenly rigid and then lurched forward like a falling telegraph pole. He too lay prone. Colonel Parkhurst looked at Tom in an unbelieving way. Before either Parkhurst or Tom could say anything, Roger was out walking across the snow. He got to where the young officer lay, wobbled and then crumpled as if his legs had turned to jelly. Looking apprehensive but thinking himself immune, Colonel Parkhurst set out after him, but fell as if poleaxed. There they lay in the virgin snow, as if posed to represent some famous ambush or massacre.

Tom strode briskly over to Hosiah, 'Give me a hand Ho'.'

Hosiah climbed down, 'Cold night Tom. A little too much cider n' gin, an' a quick walk, is all it takes to set a man up for a good night's sleep. These fellows don't seem to know these things, do they Tom?'

Together they picked up each of the men as if they were sacks of potatoes and lifted them onto the back of the farm cart. Hosiah climbed back into the driver's seat.

As Tom called out, 'Drop 'em home Hosiah, drop 'em home,' you could hear the laughter in his voice.

'Hup', Hosiah muttered. There was a creak, as first the horse and then the cart rolled slowly forwards. Colonel Parkhurst's head nodded insensibly with each bumpy motion.

(near Brent Knoll)

Cider Memories

Mooching for Apples

When I was a young man. Still at home with mum and dad in their cottage, a neighbour of ours used to make his own cider. He was the last of a long line of farmers and he had a tumble-down old cider house, with a proper mill and press and everything. He used to make his cider all on his own. He had one problem though, he only had a few apple trees and he never looked after them at all. It was rare they gave him good crop. Well, he was a bit mean, and there's nothing apple trees hate more than meanness. As soon as he passed on, well, I've never seen so many juicy red apples.

Anyway, every year, when he realised he didn't have enough apples of his own, he used to mooch round to all the neighbours, whinging and wheedling for windfalls, 'Have you got any spare apples mam? I'd be much obliged.' Often, for a laugh, my sister and I used to fetch him all the maggoty and bruised ones from under our trees. Some folks said they'd seen him at night, scrumping his neighbours' apples and hiding them under his tatty old coat.

Each year when he'd made his cider, to his credit, he used to fetch a bottle round to all the neighbours who'd donated apples.

What was it like? Well it was horrible, like vinegar with bits of mouldy apple floating it. Mother used to clean the windows with it. I expect it would've cleared the drains too, if we'd tried it.

(Not far from Bath)

What You Can Do With Cider

You can use cider for everything! There's cider cake, with apples in it too. Cider chutney with raisins and ginger for putting on poultry, pork or fish. Cider pasties are just right too. Mash your cider in with the spuds n' swedes. It's also the best flavouring for a beef and onion pie.

You should cook with it too. Poach your cod in cider, or better still congar! You can even roast in cider, either pork or beef. Don't put fat in your baking tray, just cider, sweet or dry, whatever your taste. It spices up a poor joint, and helps tenderise a tough one, and while your meat's roasting, baste with it too. Pigeon breasts roasted in cider make a meal fit for a king.

When you do your joint in cider, put your 'tatties in it too. Beautiful.

Always pour a cup or so of cider into a rabbit stew. I know people who jug hare or rabbit in cider. Myself, I'd rather not eat hare. I like to keep my luck in.

It does deserts too! A cider trifle is a delight after a Sunday roast.

I can remember my old mum washing up stubborn pans and plates with some of the rough! It soon cut through the grease it did. Better than a lemon.

(Burnham-on-Sea)

Great Grandma's 'Medicine'

My mum's family come from the Mendips, and go back a long way. It seems that lethal homebrew is a tradition all over Somerset. My great grandmother was extremely proud of her homemade 'medicine'. She turned every sort of fruit into alcohol, not just apples. When my mother, who had been coerced into 'signing the pledge' as a child, refused to sample a brew, her grandmother said; 'That's not alcohol. It's just fruit juice'.

Great grandmother's greatest brewing success, occurred the day the doctor was called to the house. After he had seen to his business, she proudly convinced him to sample various remedies from her own 'apothecary's cabinet'. He left in very good spirits, but did not return home and a search party was sent out. He was found later that day, sleeping it off on the grass verge by the side of the road, having fallen off his horse. His horse was happily cropping the grass beside him.

(Julia Day, Milverton)

Moonshine

Potato whisky isn't the only moonshine or illegal spirit brewed by the Irish. Some of them old country boys would distil anything to get a bit of fire in them. The older farmers would often make rough cider out of any old apples and fruit, just to distil it and make applejack. That's what the French call calvados and in Somerset you call cider brandy.

By the way, do you know where moonshine got its name from. Well I'll tell you. The first time you taste it you're given a glassful, and you're told to down it in one, mainly because it tastes like hot coals. Anyway, you tip it down your neck, and the next thing you know you're lying on your back staring up at the sky, and the moon's shining.

A friend of mine, Neil, a man of few words, who had a lovely wife named Ruth, dark haired, blue eyed, with a whispy girlish figure, got the idea of making his own applejack, and he built a special shed for it, right down the end of his garden by the privy. When he gave me a tour, it was frightening. He had an old iron stove in there, glass vials, copper pans, bubbling vats and plenty of stone jars full of home-made rough cider. There were pipes connecting this to that, and that to this, and steam puffing everywhere. He seemed proud but I couldn't wait to get out. It was so hot!

A week later I went back to see how he was getting on. His wife, a sensitive sort, took me out into the back garden and led me down to his shed. There was plenty of black smoke coming out of the shed chimney, but he wouldn't respond to our knocks on the door, or his wife's calling. We waited. I suppose we both assumed he was in the middle of some vital alchemical operation. While she was apologising for his rudeness I began to notice a sort of vibration creeping up through my legs. The smoke from the shed chimney was growing blacker and blacker. I thought it my imagination at first, but the whole shed was beginning to shake.

'Ruth', I said as calmly as possible, 'I think we should go and wait up the other end of the garden.'

I pushed and prodded her up the path and put myself between her and the shed. The explosion was deafening and as we turned we saw bits of wood and old aluminium saucepans raining out of the sky. Ruth just turned, looked at me and started crying. I stared up, waiting for parts of Neil to begin to fall to earth.

We heard a slam and a white faced Neil emerged from the privy frantically buttoning up his trousers. Ruth screamed and ran towards him as if he was Lazarus risen from the tomb.

All Neil ever said about the incident was, 'A very sound cure for a nasty bout of constipation.'

(Irish Bob)

Pixies, Ghosts and Witchcraft

The Parson's Nose

This was a story told to me by my father, a farmer born and bred up on Mendip. Up until the war we always made and drunk our own cider, and dad was very proud to offer guests a cup of the best from our own orchards, and what with a slice of ham and a chunk of cheddar, they were usually well pleased come the end of the evening.

One autumn, word reached us that the village's new vicar was visiting the outlying farms one by one, checking on his flock, and that he was fond of 'homely entertainment'. Sure enough, he sent word to us of his impending visit, and duly arrived one blustery evening. We had a huge fire blazing in the grate, the old oak settle pulled up close to it, and a spread fit for twenty on the kitchen table. We ate as a family, dad at the table's head, the vicar on his right hand side, with my two sisters and I further away. Mother was in and out of the kitchen seeing to this and that, and keeping the cider flowing. The vicar was a tall dark-haired man, quite young, but his penchant for good living, was beginning to show in a stomach bulging under his waistcoat.

Meal over, dad and the vicar took to the settle and drank more cider in the heat of the fire. 'Cider!' dad kept calling, and mother would leave whatever she was doing and pour them more. Eventually we all went to bed and left the men to it.

Dad told us the tale the next day. They drank on into the small hours, the vicar growing redder around the gills, and progressively loosening that bulging waistcoat, until finally dad stood up and announced, 'Right I'm for bed and it would be a bad host that didn't show his guest to the farm gate.'

The vicar stood up a little wobbly on his feet, and shook hands, all smiles, 'I wouldn't dream of forcing you out into the cold on such a night. You've been most kind as it is, a true gentleman.'

'It can be tricky to find your way in the dark, there's no lights for miles around.'

The vicar shook his head, 'Oh no, I'll be fine. I'll follow my nose.' He tapped the side of his very red snout.

After a few more goodbyes he left. Dad stood at the door and watched him for a while. Once he'd gone a hundred yards or so, he began to weave a little. Dad smiled to himself, shut the door and went back to the fire to smoke his pipe.

The rest of the tale is legendary, and here it is as told to my dad by the vicar himself:

'It was blowing a storm, wind howling, leaves flying around me. I got down to the bottom of the farm drive and passed through the gate, making sure it was shut behind me. I went right, back towards the village. All I could see in the darkness was the hedges and tumble down stone walls on either side of the lane. I knew that after the lane veered to the right, the second gate would take me into a certain field, and if I crossed that field it would take me to the lane that leads to the vicarage.

I found that old gate and went into the field. It has been left to grass and was a little muddy. All I had to do was march straight across it to the other gate directly opposite. Off I went, only when I reached the opposite side of the field there was no gate, only hedging swaying in the wind. I walked a few yards to my right, no luck. Then to my left, no luck. I walked right along that side of the field, still no gate. I was sure it was the right field for my shortcut, so I reasoned that what with all that cider, I had walked diagonally and was on the wrong side of the field. Determined to find that gate, I followed the hedge stumbling in the dark. It was some walk, that's a three acre field. Eventually I reached the corner and turned, still following the hedge. I kept on and on, walking fast, growing quite out of breath. I began to worry when I reached a second corner. I kept going though, thinking that I'd soon reach the gate I had entered by. I didn't, I reached another field corner and turned again. I'd rather you didn't tell anyone, but I began to panic a little and started to run.

I reached another corner of the field and stopped to get my wind. I was dispirited, believing I had missed both gates in the dark. I even suspected someone of playing a joke on me and moving them, but that would have been impossible. I kept on walking, tripping on grassy mounds and dips. I turned another corner, then another. Two or three times I must have rounded that field. I felt embarrassed and aware what I must have looked like to anyone who was watching me. I even felt there were eyes on me nearby. I stopped once or twice and shouted, 'You can come out now, I've had enough. I give up.' But there was no answer, just the rustling of leaves, which in my tired mind, sounded a little like laughter.

I walked another side of the field and not finding the gate, totally downhearted, I collapsed in the wet grass, feeling that as I was unable to get home, I might as well sleep there as anywhere. My head swam a little, my legs were tired from walking, and my eyes felt heavy. Thinking of no better strategy I took off my coat and jacket and unbuttoned my waistcoat, endeavouring to make myself a little more comfortable. Then I had a change of heart. I couldn't fall asleep unprotected in a field and risk catching a chill, or worse still, someone finding me sleeping off the cider, out in the open, in the morning. I put my jacket back on and then my coat. When I tried to button it, I found I'd put it on inside out. I whipped it off again and as I did so, I saw the old gate I'd been searching for all along. Filled with joy I ran to it and nearly hugged it. I got home with no further mishaps.'

My dad, when he'd stopped laughing, fixed him with a serious stare, 'You were pixillated. Led astray by the pixies. It hasn't happened to anyone round here for years, but there you are. It's lucky you knew what to do. It takes a wise man to know that the only way to release himself from a pixy's spell, is to take off his jacket and put it on inside out.'

The vicar looked around them to make sure no one else was listening and whispered, 'I don't believe in such things. It must have been your cider.'

Dad just smiled, and said, 'Well when you're near the farm, I do hope you drop in for glass or two.'

(Near Blagdon)

The Apple Tree Pixy

In my parent's garden, at the far end beyond the roses, there was an old apple tree, a cooker. One night I arrived home late after having a drink or two, and stood in the kitchen looking out of the window into the dark of the garden. I was not feeling at all drunk, but I filled a glass from the tap and slowly drank the water, still gazing out at the old apple tree. Something unusual caught my eye. On one of the main branches, to the tree's right, there was an unusual shape, a perfect black silhouette of a small man sitting facing me, with his legs dangling from the branch, and his left arm raised holding onto a side branch. I could make out a Phrygian type cap, not a tall one like a garden gnome's, and he had a very round head.

Thinking he was a chance shape formed of one or two branches and an old apple, I continued staring but moved right to one end of the window. He was still there. I moved back to the other end of the window. He was still there. I tried blinking, still there. Then I shut my eyes and counted to ten. On opening them, I began to feel odd. He was still there. I continued staring, and thought of going out into the garden for a closer look, but I felt oddly frozen as if I just couldn't do that. I took another long look at the apple tree pixy and then went to bed, resolving to go out into the garden for a closer look in the morning.

In the morning light, the branch he had sat on, and the side branch he had held onto were real enough, but empty.

(Taplow, Berkshire)

107

A Chance Encounter

My brother and I had been testing out the cider at one of the village public houses. We said our goodbyes and I set off, aiming to clear my head by walking through the brisk autumn night. I decided to take a shortcut over the land belonging to the farm I was then working on. My path took me through two meadow fields and into the old orchard. The grass was wet underfoot and the yellowing leaves were clinging to my boots as I walked.

I wasn't the worse for wear, just a little 'bright.' Anyway, I climbed the gate from the last meadow into the orchard, steady enough, and was soon among the trees. It was growing rather misty and I hugged my jacket tight about me to help keep out the damp.

Those old trees leaned this way and that. Some of them had their huge thick branches propped up on stakes of wood driven deep into the ground. The air smelled of apples and there was windfalls underfoot. Several of them nearly had me over in the dark. I had to keep looking down at my footing, and then up to check I was travelling in the right direction.

I don't scare easy and I'm not one for pixies and such like, But I got a feeling on me that something, perhaps an animal, was watching me from behind a tree somewhere. Now, there's always odd scurryings and noises in the countryside after dark, and I'm used to them, but every now and then I thought I heard something big moving somewhere close by, so any minute I almost expected to come on a fat old badger scrumping windfalls.

Halfway through the orchard I saw a tall shadow moving up ahead. I wasn't sure at first, as it vanished behind a tree. Then I saw it again and my heart was my mouth. There's some poachers, real rogues, that it's very unwise to disturb, but I reasoned it was more likely to be the farmer, up and about to see who I was and what I was up to. I straightened up, trying to look as if I had every right to be walking by night. The shape grew darker as it got nearer, but in the mist I couldn't see who it was until we were almost passing.

I'll swear to any man who cares to listen, that what I describe now is what I saw. I made out a very smart black dress suit. You know, top hat and tails, black tie, cane with a silver head and shining patent shoes. I almost laughed at the thought of some fine gentleman running into me in an orchard at midnight, but there was something else odd about him. Even accounting for his top hat he was a sight shorter than me. Then, when I looked into his face I came over all queasy. I was looking at a fox. He sort of licked his lips and smiled. Our eyes met, and I was gazing amazed, into a pair of flecked amber eyes.

And I swear this is what happened next. He tipped his hat to me, and what's more he did it with a fox's paw. 'Good evening,' he said in a sort of husky voice.

'Evening,' I replied and hurried on. I did not dare look back, and as soon as I was a dignified distance away, I don't mind admitting, I ran, even though my legs were wobbling like jellies on a plate.

I've never seen anything like it since, and you won't catch me in that orchard ever again.

(Taunton Vale)

Interestingly, there are many Chinese legends and folktales about fox faeries, beings that can shapeshift into and out of human form.

The Love Apple

When I was a young girl growing up in the countryside, we were very poor, but I remember it as a happy time. I used to share the attic bedroom in our cottage with my two sisters, Jessie and Norma. I was the eldest, and when I turned sixteen I went and fell in love with one of the young men who used to work with my father out on the farm - very handsome. I would sit and wait for him to pass, and try and smile at him, but mostly I hid my face in embarrassment.

Jessie could be sweet but she was also a parcel of mischief. She ran up to this lad, Ben his name was, and told him I 'had an eye to him.'

I could have died of fright and shame. I wasn't the most confident young woman. Still, it turns out she did me a favour. The next day I was sitting outside our cottage shelling peas for the dinner, daydreaming as usual, when I heard footsteps. Before I could look up, he was there standing in front of me, holding out something in his hand. 'For you.' he said. His face was bright red. He was as embarrassed as me. It was Ben holding out a juicy red apple. Hardly daring to look at him I took it and muttered, 'Thank you.'

He walked away so quickly he almost ran.

That night, when Jessie, Norma and I were up in our attic room, in our night-dresses with our hair brushed ready for bed, I told them what had happened.

'What did it taste like?' Jessie giggled.

I shook my head and held out the apple for them both to see.

'I would have eaten it straight away,' Jessie laughed, 'He must love you too you know.'

'Don't listen to her,' Norma advised, 'she doesn't understand these things. You've got to keep that apple, then it'll be a magic spell, a love spell.'

'What do you mean?' I asked.

'Put it under your bed, under where your heart is when you sleep, and it'll make sure he'll always be true to you.'

'I'll do it if you make Jessie promise not to move it for a prank.'

She promised and I made the spell. Of course, I forgot all about the apple, but in a year or two Ben and I were married and I left home. The other two girls went their ways not long after me, and our parents stayed there all their days.

Dad passed first and then mum, and it was left to me to sort out the old cottage. Being a sentimental old thing, dear old mum had left our room in the attic exactly as it was when we lived there, just in case any of us needed to return in an emergency.

I was upstairs cleaning that dusty old place, and I wasn't thinking of any such thing, but I checked under each bed and there, under mine, was a strange little hard brown ball. I picked it up and peered at its wizened skin before I realised what it was - my apple! And after fifty years it was still whole, dried and smaller, but whole. Perhaps it was the air in the attic that had preserved it. Either that or the love with which it was given. Whatever it was, for sixty years, until he passed on, Ben stayed true to me.

What's more I've still got that apple here with me. It's under my bed!

(old people's home near Wells)

A Fair Trade

I was only fourteen or fifteen years old, and it was the summer holidays. What's more, my luck was in. My dad had come into some money and had splashed out on a new bike for me. Just the one I wanted, a red Raleigh, fitted out with a dynamo. And if you don't remember, a dynamo was a gadget that you put on your bike to power the front and back lights, instead of batteries. It worked by using pedal power to produce electricity. The faster you pedalled the brighter your lights shone. The only snag was that when you stopped at traffic lights, your lights went out and no one could see you! It was the latest technology.

I got myself a summer job helping out one of our old neighbours, Jack Holland. A fine old countryman, who'd spent his life working on the farm and various local shoots. Sadly, his cottage was becoming too much for him to manage, and he was moving to a smaller bungalow nearby. My role was to help him clean it and clear out the junk he'd accumulated in sixty years of hoarding. Some if it had been his dad's!

Right from the start, I had my eye on the fine pair of red deer antlers that hung in his front room. I knew he wouldn't find a place for them in his new home. After three weeks of toil I confessed my desire. He grinned a wry smile and thought a moment, 'It would be a pleasure. You can take them next Saturday when you finish here'.

That Saturday morning I pedalled faster then usual to get to Jack's cottage. It didn't go as planned. The last box of belongings wasn't taped up until darkness was drawing on. I was getting more and more impatient. It didn't help that Jack had been at the cider since three o'clock and was less than sober. 'Come and have a drink my lad. I've got to finish this cider before I move. The removal men might spill it'.

He was upset, and so I joined him. The cider went down well and we talked and talked, stories of the moor, ghosts and pheasants, and cider and wrestling. We talked of everything. When Jack felt fortified and able to face bed and his move the next day, I rose to leave. My knees buckled a little and things were swirly, but I stayed standing.

'Your antlers.' He had fetched them down and left them out for me, complete with a ball of string to strap them to my bike.

Of course, they wouldn't fit anywhere, and we were giggling together like old comrades. Jack thought a while and was inspired with the solution, 'Shut your eyes boy and I'll sort it properly.'

He was fumbling and chuckling, and then I felt string being wound around my head. He was tying the antlers to my head. They seemed to weigh a ton and I had trouble keeping my head up. Eventually I felt him back off and roar with amusement. 'You're enough to frighten an old man.' He held up a little mirror, and I saw a strange bleary eyed vision, head bound haphazardly with string, and sporting a huge pair of antlers, that protruded a good two foot either side of his head.

We said our goodbyes and I set off wobbling on my bike, dynamo powered lights flickering from my irregular pedalling. I had only a few twists and turns to negotiate, then it was a long coast downhill to my mum and dad's place. I found it hard going. I turned the last corner and began to pick up speed as the road dipped. The wind whistled in my antlers, and they dragged in the air, making me swerve from side to side.

Our next door neighbours were two unmarried sisters, both in their fifties and very religious, proper churchgoers, who frowned on nearly everything teenage boys enjoyed. They had a custom of going for a stroll of an evening, and that night was no exception. Ahead of me I could make out their two frumpy figures coming towards me, and in the still night air I could make out their voices. By now I was going far too fast to stop and was merrily careering from one side of the narrow road to the other.

'What are those lights Mary?'

'I don't like it Judith. It's not right.'

'What shall we do?'

'Just keep walking.'

I had started laughing and tears were streaming down my face and I was wobbling more than ever, dynamo blazing. Then they saw me. 'Mary, oh my God it's the Devil.'

'Don't blaspheme.'

'But look!'

'In the Lord's name it's him. What shall we do?

'He's come for us. You must have done something wrong.'

'Don't blame me. It's your wickedness got us into this.'

I was speeding towards them, trying not to think of the consequences of knocking them both over, petticoats flying.

By now they were squealing, 'The Devil! The Devil!'

I missed them by an inch, swerved off the road and tipped over into the ditch on the right hand side. I was lying on my back, feet in the air, antlers pinning my head to the ground. To my horror I heard footsteps. They were coming to investigate.

'Mary don't go near.'

'Suppose he's hurt?'

'Don't be silly, it's the Devil.'

They were soon standing over me, white-faced, clutching each other in fear. 'Oh look Mary, he's got a new bike with a dynamo.'

'Don't have any sympathy for him Judith. Can you smell that, the evil old thing's been at the cider!'

(Exmoor)

Wildlife Tales

An Inventive Rat

You won't believe this but it's true. When my old mum was still alive and living here in the cottage with my wife and I, she was in charge of the chickens and various chores around the yard and garden.

One morning, the wife was out on an errand in the village and mum was in the yard. She let out a terrific yell, 'Geoffrey!'

I was there in a flash. She was pointing at a hole in the bottom of the old wooden door that led into one of our store buildings, 'I saw a rat go in there through that hole.'

We went back in the house and I got my shotgun. A bit drastic perhaps, but a good blast would reassure mum.

I waited there for a while, hidden behind a barrel, staring hard down the sites of my gun. After about ten minutes there was a scraping and shuffling, and a rat came out backwards, seemingly walking on his hind legs. He turned round, and blow me, he was standing upright because he was holding a huge apple in his front paws, for all the world like a little old man carrying a medicine ball. He was keeping it steady by pressing his front teeth into it. As I watched he waddled slowly away from the door. I just watched him go. I take my hat off to any creature that ingenious, rat or whatever.

When I was sure he'd gone I fired my gun into the air. Just to put mum's mind at rest.

(Blackdown Hills)

Rook

We always encourage the rooks into our garden. They bring nothing but luck. In the summer, the new brood of youngsters always spend time poking around the flowerbeds and lawns. Once the fruit's ripe, they make the most of it. One morning as I watching from the kitchen window, a baby rook was enjoying a windfall apple so much, that he managed to impale it on his beak. It was stuck there, as if someone had pushed it onto his long beak to keep him quiet. At first he seemed a little distressed and shook his head, but it was to no avail, the apple stayed where it was. He lifted his head up and paused, thinking. In a few seconds, he had regained his dignity and hit on a cunning face saving scheme. Rather proudly, he strutted around with it for a while, trying to hold is head high as if it was all a totally intentional part of his plan for the day. Finally, when he felt the apple slipping, he dislodged it by banging it as hard as he could on the grass.

(near Watchet)

Finished Liverpool
27. July 2013

117

Bibliography of Major Sources

The Somerset Yearbook 1922 - 1939 (Folk Press Ltd)

Somerset Folklore, Ruth Tongue (The Folklore Society 1965)

Poems (inc. 'Cyder'), John Philips (T. Davies 1776)

The Customs, Superstitions, and Legends of the County of Somerset, C. H. Poole (The Toucan Press 1970)

Plant Lore, Legends, and Lyrics, Richard Folkard, Jun. (R. Folkard and Son 1884)

The Book of Crafts and Character, Walter Raymond (J. M. Dent & Sons 1934)

The Book of Simple Delights, Walter Raymond (Hodder and Stoughton 1907)

Calendar of Customs, Superstitions, Weather-lore, Popular Sayings and Important Events connected with the County of Somerset, W. G. Willis Watson, F. R. Hist. S. (1920)

A Calendar of Country Customs, Ralph Whitlock (B. T. Batlock Ltd 1978)

So Merry Let Us Be - The Living Tradition of Somerset Cider, Philippa Legg (Somerset County Council Library Service 1986)

Cidermaking, Michael B. Quinion, (Shire Pub. Ltd 1982)

The Origin and Meaning of Apple Cults, James Rendel Harris (1918)

Norse Poems, W. H. Auden and Paul B. Taylor (Faber and Faber 1983)

Mastering Herbalism, Paul Huson (Stein and Day 1983)

A Somerset Journal, Berta Lawrence (Westaway Books 1951)

Modern Herbal, Mrs M. Grieve (Penguin Books Ltd 1978)

Exmoor Custom and Song, R.W. Patten (The Exmoor Press 1974)

Glowing Embers from a Somerset Hearth, J. A. Garton (The Cathedral Press 1936)

Byegone Somerset, Editor Cumin Walters, see '*Cider Songs and Customs*,' Mrs. Burgess (1897)

General View of the Agriculture of the County of Somerset, John Billingsley Esq (1795)

A Somerset Pomona, The Cider Apples of Somerset, Liz Copas (The Dovecote Press 2001)

Ogham - Wisdom of the Trees, Jon Dathen (Capall Bann Publishing 2003)

Greek Lyric Poetry, (Sappho poem) Translator Willis Barnstone (Bantam Books 1962)

Virgil - The Pastoral Poems, (The Eclogues), Translator E. V. Rieu (Penguin Books Ltd 1949)

Special thanks to all those individuals who gave verbal testimonies.

Other titles from Capall Bann:

Flower Wisdom - The definitive guidebook to the myth, magic and mystery of flowers   by Katherine Kear

From the poppies of Flanders - symbols of sleep and oblivion - to the purity of the lily and the faery associations of the daisy, flowers have always been surrounded by myths, magic and mystery. This illustrated guide explores the physical and symbolic properties of the best known and loved flowers of the Western hemisphere, including the bluebell, lily, anemone, poppy, daffodil, iris and rose. Each is described in terms of its botanical properties, its origins, the folklore and history that surrounds it, and how it is used for health and well-being. All plants are inextricably linked to the science, culture, religion and economics of the world. Some are used to heal, others become symbols for worship, Flowers can indicate political allegiance, romantic passion, sympathy and social class. They are universal symbols of ephemerability and purity, and of the natural cycles of birth, death and regeneration. Packed with a wealth of information, this is a unique guide to the myth, magic and wisdom of flowers. ISBN 186163 237 1   £14.95

Real Fairies   by David Tame

"Here we have first-hand accounts....reliable witnesses....Highly recommended!"
The Cauldron *"sure to be of interest'* The Fairy Ring   *"a fascinating read"* Silver Wheel
Encounters with fairies seem to be increasing. This book relates the experiences of many people, some famous (such as BBC presenter Valerie Singleton), some clairvoyant, some everyday, who have seen and met members of the fairy kingdom. It appears that our world and theirs are drawing closer together again and it is possible for more and more people to see real fairies. ISBN 186163 0719   £9.95

The Fairies in the Irish Tradition   by Molly Gowen

"....a highly recommended book for those who love fairy lore and will make a lovely addition to your fairy library.....captivating and charming....a comprehensive study of the fairy nature and its manifestation in the Irish Tradition." Fairy Tales

Illustrated with stories and legends and illuminated with superb artwork. Contents include: Fairy Nature - fallen angels, elementals and ghosts; Fairies in the Landscape; The Banshee; History of the Sidhe; the Fairy Doctor; Tir na nOg; magical animals, the Pooka, the King of Cats and Demon Dogs. Many superb illustrations by Lavinia Hamer. ISBN 186163 0859   £7.95

The Mythology of the Mermaid and Her Kin   by Marc Potts

"Most welcome...beautifully illustrated, with the author's unique artwork this is an excellent study of a neglected aspect of folklore and mythology. Highly recommended" The Cauldron

Explores the origin of Mermaids and Mermen. Sea deities, especially those depicted as being fish-tailed are explored, as is the mythology of woman's association with water. The folklore of mermaids is related, especially from Britain and Northern Europe, with relevant examples from other parts of the world. Other topics related include: the mermaid's image in bestiaries, the mermaid and the Christian church, carvings and heraldry, recorded sightings and captures, the seal/siren explanation, mermaid hoaxes and the mermaids' image today.   Beautifully illustrated by Marc's renowned artwork. ISBN 186163 0395   £10.95

Gardening For Wildlife   Ron Wilson

"If you have only one wildlife book, this is the one to have. The information contained in this book is invaluable. A very interesting read for young and old alike, to which you will always refer." The Professional Gardener   *"..a real delight...a fascinating read...all of the methods I have tried so far have gleaned superb results"* Touchstone   *"lively, colloquial style...quick and easy to read...inspiring and full of helpful tips'* Place
"..a nice book...lively drawings which clearly illustrate techniques...covers everything...a good starter book" Permaculture
A few 'modifications' and additions could enhance the value of most gardens for wildlife. That is what this book is all about. It offers practical advice and ideas for improvements and where possible suggests the inclusion of 'extra' features which will support and encourage a rich diversity of plant, insect, bird and animal life. Plants, foods and features are all described in plain English. Everything in this book is explained in straightforward terms to enable anyone to help their local wildlife. ISBN 1 86163 011 5   £10.95   Illustrated

In Pursuit of Perennial Profit - The Pot of Gold at the Bottom of the Garden   Patrick Vickery

Shows how to make your garden productive in a variety of ways, for both expert and gardening novice alike, at minimum cost and in an innovative and self-financing way. For those who know little or nothing about gardening this will start you on your way - a journey of discovery and self-fulfilment. Choosing plants to grow, organising time and space (you don't need much of either!), deterring slugs, getting the best from the plants and even how to sell excess plants should you wish are all covered here. The author writes from real experience, growing plants in the not always ideal location of Ross-shire in Scotland, as he says '"if I can do it, anybody can". ISBN 186163 1480 £7.95

The Way the Cookie Crumbles   Malcolm Kidd

"...source of considerable interest.... lively confessions.... strong thread of humour.... hearty laughter inspired by minor misfortunes and amiable eccentricities." The Keswick Reminder
Introducing himself as a "mail order cattle salesman" - in addition to farming, Malcolm Kidd has had a full and colourful life, meeting 'worthies' and rogues in abundance. He describes his boyhood on the farm, and six wartime years in the army where he managed to start at the top and work his way down! Country tales of local squires, gamekeepers and poachers are nostalgic and often humourous. The book is illustrated with numerous period photographs. ISBN 186163 1529 £10.95

The Subterranean Kingdom
- A Survey of Man-made Structures Beneath the Earth   Nigel Pennick

Cave dwellings, catacombs, earth houses, rock-cut temples, tombs, hermitages, tunnels and mines - these are just a few of the fascinating and mysterious subterranean structures that are uncovered and described in this unique history. Nigel Pennick traces the history and use of subterranea and explores the myths and legends that they have inspired. This panoramic survey includes the legend of the vast tunnel system beneath the Andes, the majestic and awesome Oracle of the Dead at Baiae, the Hellfire Club of Sir Francis Dashwood, the secret underground city of Ivan the Terrible and a concise guide to British subterranea.
ISBN 186163 073 5   £12.95

FREE DETAILED CATALOGUE

Capall Bann is owned and run by people actively involved in many of the areas in which we publish. A detailed illustrated catalogue is available on request, SAE or International Postal Coupon appreciated. **Titles can be ordered direct from Capall Bann, post free in the UK** (cheque or PO with order) or from good bookshops and specialist outlets.

FREE detailed catalogue Contact:
Capall Bann Publishing, Auton Farm, Milverton, Somerset, TA4 1NE